IMAGES
of America

MOUNTAIN HOME AIR FORCE BASE

The base has always had a good relationship with the neighboring town of Mountain Home, the city from which the base took its name. For this reason, the outpost has always adorned one of its jets with the title "City of Mountain Home." In 1954, the 9th Bombardment Wing, the host unit of the base at the time, christened the first B-47 the "Spirit of Idaho," and LaVonne Stalsky, Miss Idaho, broke a bottle of Snake River water over the airplane's nose.

On the Cover: This photograph was taken of the 480th Tactical Fighter Squadron while it was stationed at Da Nang Air Base, South Vietnam. In 1967, the 366th Tactical Fighter Wing was not part of Mountain Home's history, but the photograph is significant in the fact that it shows the unit's unofficial crest, the gunfighter. For years, when airmen spoke of being stationed at Mountain Home Air Force Base, most automatically thought him to be a gunfighter. The word has become synonymous with Mountain Home's history, and for this reason, the author thought it only apt to show a photograph that depicts the origin of that coveted emblem. (Photograph courtesy of the U.S. Air Force.)

Yancy D. Mailes

ISBN 978-0-7385-4805-0

Published by Arcadia Publishing
Charleston SC, Chicago IL, Portsmouth NH, San Francisco CA

Printed in the United States of America

Library of Congress Catalog Card Number: 2007924635

For all general information contact Arcadia Publishing at:
Telephone 843-853-2070
Fax 843-853-0044
E-mail sales@arcadiapublishing.com
For customer service and orders:
Toll-Free 1-888-313-2665

Visit us on the Internet at www.arcadiapublishing.com

To those who have endured the rigors of serving at Mountain Home.

Contents

ACKNOWLEDGMENTS

This project was a monumental task and one I could not have completed without the assistance of many giving people. I would like to thank the following individuals, whose contributions made the completion of this book possible. First, Gary Boyd made me aware of his Arcadia project and encouraged me to pursue my own. Second, I would like to send a healthy thank you to Master Sergeant Tom Lauria for combing the archives at Maxwell Air Force Base, Alabama, and scanning the excellent World War II images. I still owe you that bottle of whiskey. Next, Joe Eastman spent a tremendous amount of time scanning damaged negatives, making the end products look fabulous. Gary Keith of the Idaho Military Historical Society opened his archives and allowed me to pull items relating to Mountain Home's history. In the absence of World War II construction photographs, I made a giant leap of faith and found Joe Terteling via the Internet. Joe is the son of Joseph W. Terteling, the man who, along with his brother, helped build Mountain Home Army Air Field. Joe went above and beyond to find the "E" award photographs as well as a handful of construction snapshots. Joe, thank you very much, you made this project shine, and it now tells your father's history much better than it ever would have without your help. Airman First Class Ryan Crane printed close to 100 photographs, allowing me to rescan the images into Tiffs. My counterpart, Master Sergeant Mike Sibley, acted as a sounding board while giving me honest feedback on the book. I would also like to thank Aldo Panzieri for allowing me to use his photographs. Aldo was a photographer here at Mountain Home in the mid-1960s, and he captured the day-to-day lives of the military very well. Lastly, I want to thank my lovely wife, Lisa, for the countless hours I spend in my own little world. I appreciate your patience and your counsel. You are my rock.

Introduction

When reflecting on Mountain Home Air Force Base (AFB), one automatically ponders the Gunfighters. This is natural, because the 366th has been Mountain Home's longest-serving tenant, as well as its latest resident. However, long before the Gunfighters planted roots in the Gem State, Mountain Home served as a waypoint for many other groups leaving their mark on the air force's history.

In 1942, the U.S. Army Air Corps training program touched Mountain Home for the first time. On June 20, 1942, the district engineer of the U.S. Army Corps of Engineers at Portland, Oregon, received instruction by the division engineer and the commanding general of the 2nd Air Force to investigate the prospect of building an air base near Jerome, Idaho. After some exploration, the engineers suggested a site some 10 miles southwest of the town of Mountain Home, Idaho. The proposed location, consisting of barren, undeveloped, low-priced ($1–$2 an acre) land, offered engineering advantages that would substantially reduce both construction time and costs. It would require little filling and grading, and it had none of the irrigation canals and drainage ditches that characterized the developed (about $95 an acre) real estate of the Jerome location. Following the district engineer's suggestion, the Army Air Corps choose Mountain Home as the spot for a new air base.

Without delay, the district engineer contacted J. A. Terteling and Sons of Boise, Idaho, and contracted the company to build the base. The Tertelings had a good reputation for meeting tight deadlines and had worked government contracts in the past. They had established this status when they resurfaced the runway at Gowen Field, a new B-17 training base on the outskirts of Boise, Idaho. Construction began on Mountain Home on November 30, 1942, and as it progressed, more and more personnel of various support units arrived. The base drew the majority of its personnel from the 18th Replacement Wing at Salt Lake City, Utah, and the various units assigned to Gowen Field in Boise, Idaho. The first base commander, Lt. Col. Carlos L. Reavis, assumed command on January 29, 1943, but his tenure was short lived, and he relinquished command to Col. Arthur J. Melanson.

Colonel Melanson oversaw the construction of the base, which officially opened on August 7, 1943. As a B-24 training facility, the base boasted two 10,000-foot runways that ran northwest-southeast and east-west. By the end of August 1943, construction of the entire base (costing nearly $13 million) was substantially finished. Besides the runways, taxiways, and parking apron, the projects included headquarters, administrative, and classroom buildings, four hangars, an engineering shop, a hospital, a theater, multiple barracks, and several mess halls. In addition, the engineers designed and built a railroad spur from the Union Pacific track at Mountain Home to the base and a 12-mile, four-lane highway between base and town. Further, four wooden towers for celestial-navigation training were erected, the last three becoming ready in January 1944. Bombing and gunnery ranges were built in a region near the base, the largest being Saylor Creek Aerial Gunnery Range. Lastly, an on-base housing project for civilian employees was begun. Like all small communities near burgeoning wartime installations, housing in town was inadequate for military and civilian needs.

On February 16, 1943, the 2nd Air Force activated the 396th Bombardment Group (H) at Mountain Home and directed the unit to reach full strength by April 25. However, in early April, the group transferred without personnel and equipment to Moses Lake, Washington, where it became a replacement training unit for B-17 combat crews. In its place, the Army Air Force activated the 470th Bombardment Group (H) on May 1, 1943, and the unit began arriving shortly after the base became active in August. Equipped with B-24s, the 470th functioned as a replacement training unit until November, when the 20th Air Base Squadron assumed those duties. In January 1944, the 470th moved on to Tonopah, Nevada, and in its place, the 490th and 494th Bombardment Groups stood up training operations. Eventually the 490th deployed overseas to the European theater, while the 494th headed to the Pacific. For the duration of World War II, numerous B-24 units trained at Mountain Home Army Air Field, but even before the war came to a close, the Army Air Force sought a new mission for the high-desert base.

While B-24 crew training continued into June 1945, plans called for the base to convert to the new B-32 Dominator. Preparations for this change began in April 1945, with parts for the B-32 beginning to arrive and the runways undergoing minor upgrades. A portion of the training personnel at Mountain Home went to other bases and factories for familiarization with the B-32 while the B-24 program wound down. The first of seven B-32 bombers arrived at Mountain Home on May 26, but these aircraft passed through for staging, not training. The B-32 program proved short lived, with plans canceled in early June 1945 before any training could begin.

The military replaced the aborted Dominator with a B-29 Superfortress training program, and the first aircraft arrived June 23, 1945. By August, the base had 40 B-29s assigned and the first class had begun, but plans again changed as World War II ended. The sole B-29 class left Mountain Home by the end of August, and later that month, the mission reverted back to B-24 training. By October 5, 1945, the base was placed on inactive status, and most personnel returned to their home states. The process of closing down the base continued until early November, when all of the facilities were put in caretaker status.

From the end of 1945 until August 1948, responsibility for the base changed hands from Gowen Field to Walla Walla Army Air Field in Washington State. Eventually, in December 1948, a small services squadron arrived and prepared the outpost for a grand reopening as Mountain Home Air Force Base. A short time later, in May 1949, personnel of the 5th Reconnaissance Group arrived with their RB-17s and began operations. This continued for roughly one year, when on April 25, 1950, the base again was placed on inactive status and the 5th departed Mountain Home.

The base sat vacant for almost one year; then, in February 1951, the spooks of the air resupply and communications (ARC) wings arrived. As the air force's first special operations units, the men and women of the ARCs practiced for unconventional warfare while they operated SA-16 amphibious airplanes, C-119 Boxcars, and B-29s Superfortresses. From 1951 until 1953, three separate ARC units operated from the tiny field and then deployed to overseas locations. For years, this portion of Mountain Home's history went unacknowledged due to the high classification of the mission.

In May 1953, with the last ARC unit departing Mountain Home, control of the base passed to Strategic Air Command (SAC), which assigned its 9th Bombardment Wing to the base. Initially the unit operated the antiquated B-29 bomber and the KB-29 refueling aircraft but in September 1954 converted to the new B-47 bomber and the KC-97 tanker. For over a decade, the 9th acted as the host of the high-desert base and oversaw the transformation of the area from a dusty airstrip into Idaho's only SAC stronghold. As the 1950s came to a close, the air force announced it would build three Titan missile sites in Idaho and assign control of the areas to the 9th Bombardment Wing. In all, the missile sites remained active for about three years, with the sites closed in June 1965.

A few years later, the Strategic Air Command mission began to wane at Mountain Home AFB. In November 1964, the air force announced plans to close the three missile sites, and at the same time, it began phasing out the aging B-47 bomber. With this shift in mission, the 9th moved to Beale AFB, California, and on January 1, 1966, Tactical Air Command (TAC) took control and assigned the 67th Tactical Reconnaissance Wing as the host unit. The 67th flew RF-4Cs and conducted photographic, visual, radar, and thermal reconnaissance operations. In May 1966, shortly after its arrival, the 67th added RF-4C replacement training to its mission, training aircrews for assignment to overseas units. Two years later, the unit also became responsible for tactical fighter operations with the June 1968 addition of a squadron of F-4D Phantoms. This fighter mission lasted until November 1970, when TAC reassigned the F-4D forces.

In May 1971, the 347th Tactical Fighter Wing arrived at Mountain Home and replaced the 67th as the host unit. The RF-4C mission disbanded, and Mountain Home began to receive the F-111F. The 347th had a short stay at Mountain Home, as the 366th Tactical Fighter Wing—or as they are better known, the Gunfighters—arrived on October 31, 1972. As the 366th absorbed the assets of the 347th, its original three squadrons of World War II heritage (389th, 390th, and 391st) arrived to conduct F-111F operations. This continued until 1977. In order to modernize its European forces, the air force decided to send the F-111F aircraft from Mountain Home to the wing at Royal Air Field (RAF) in Lakenheath, England. The F-4 aircraft from Lakenheath went to Nellis AFB, Nevada, while the 366th received Nellis's F-111As. This three-way swap, code-named Operation Ready Switch, took place from October 1976 through August 1977.

To offset the older aircraft acquired from Ready Switch, on March 24, 1980, the air force announced plans to place two squadrons of the new EF-111A Raven electronic countermeasures aircraft at Mountain Home. At that time, only two prototype Ravens existed, operated by Detachment 3 of the Tactical Air Warfare Center and supported by the 366th. The plan called for the Gunfighters to gradually send elements of its F-111A fleet to the Grumman Aerospace Corporation for conversion to the EF-111A. The first of the wing's aircraft entered the conversion program on February 26, 1981. From then until 1985, the wing gradually sent F-111As to Grumman and received the converted EF-111As.

On July 1, 1981, the 388th Electronic Combat Squadron activated as a component of the 366th wing with a mission to receive the EF-111A and conduct training. As the wing's inventory of F-111A fighters shrank due to the conversion process, the 390th Tactical Fighter Squadron became inactivated on October 1, 1982, leaving the 389th and 391st Tactical Fighter Squadrons as the wing's F-111A units. The 390th stayed inactive for only a few weeks, however, being re-designated as the 390th Electronic Combat Squadron and activated on December 15, 1982. At that time, the air force inactivated the 388th Electronic Combat Squadron and replaced it with the 390th, which would continue as the wing's EF-111A squadron. Along the way, air force plans for a second EF-111A unit at Mountain Home changed, as an electronic combat squadron activated in England.

Operations continued unchanged throughout the late 1980s, with the wing training F-111A and EF-111A aircrews and maintaining combat readiness in both aircraft. Early in 1989, the Department of Defense announced plans for the closure of numerous military installations and a realignment of forces. Mountain Home AFB was included in the realignment portion of the plan. George AFB in California would close, with F-4 forces from George relocating to Mountain Home and joining the F-111 operation.

In December 1989, a portion of the 366th participated in Operation Just Cause, the invasion of Panama to restore democracy and oust dictator Gen. Manuel Noriega. The 390th Electronic Combat Squadron contributed a small force of EF-111A aircraft and crews to jam enemy radars during the brief invasion.

Less than a year after Just Cause, the 390th again had to fulfill its contingency role, deploying to Saudi Arabia for Operation Desert Shield in August 1990. When the war against Iraq began in January 1991, the 390th supported coalition strike aircraft. The unit jammed enemy radar defenses throughout Operation Desert Storm, returning to Mountain Home in late March 1991. For this, the unit earned an Air Force Outstanding Unit Award with Combat "V" for its role in the Gulf War.

Plans to relocate F-4s to Mountain Home were canceled in 1991, and the base was instead chosen as home for the air force's first air intervention composite wing. Late in 1991, the 366th began receiving F-16C and F-15E aircraft for its new composite force, replacing the F-111A, which had retired. In preparation for its new mission, the 366th Tactical Fighter Wing was re-designated as the 366th Wing on October 1, 1991. In 1992, the wing added the F-15C fighter and the KC-135 tanker to its composite forces operating from Mountain Home. In addition, the 34th Bomb Squadron activated at Castle AFB, California, as a geographically separated component of the 366th Wing. However, in April 1994, the unit transferred its flag to Ellsworth AFB, South Dakota, where it began training with the B-1B Lancer. In June 1996, the 34th slowly began relocating to Mountain Home, and on April 1, 1997, the squadron transferred its flag to join the rest of the wing. By the summer of 1997, the air force's only composite wing operating five separate aircraft types began to train from Mountain Home.

On September 11, 2001, the Gunfighters sat ready to answer the nation's call. As the 911 on-call force, the wing deployed to three separate locations around the world to support Operation Enduring Freedom. The 34th deployed to Diego Garcia and opened the war on October 7, 2001, when its squadron commander led the first bombing missions. A large base-operating support force deployed to Al Undeid, Qatar, and built the dusty airstrip into what is now the premier airbase in Southwest Asia. Within one week, the group began receiving aircraft and operating the 389th's F-16s. The 391st deployed its F-15Es to a classified location, setting world records for the longest combat sortie as well as redefining the role of the Strike Eagle. In all, the 366th deployed more people and delivered more ordnance than any other conventional unit in the military.

Following the wing's return from Southwest Asia, the air force began consolidating its B-1B and KC-135 forces. This led to the reallocation of the wing's bombers and tankers to bases around the world. Following the departure of these assets, the air force re-designated the 366th as a fighter wing. With these changes, the wing's 10-year mission as the air force's only standing air expeditionary wing came to an end.

Over the next few years, Mountain Home supported the war on terror with its three original squadrons. In late 2005, the air force announced that the base would transfer its F-16s and F-15Cs and transition into an F-15E super base. As of March 2007, the transition had begun, with the 389th shipping its F-16s to other units throughout the air force.

One

The Liberators

In 1943, when people traversed the 10-mile stretch of road between the town of Mountain Home and the base, they would enjoy a view of endless miles of sagebrush broken with the occasional jackrabbit. At the end of that boring journey, they would be met by army military police guarding this gate made from indigenous volcanic rock and raw-cut planking. The portal where all passed through to enter Mountain Home Air Base has changed throughout the years but stands as solemn reminder of the military presence just a short 10 miles down the road from the town of Mountain Home. In this photograph taken in July 1943, the gate guards have clearly made a statement on what cannot be brought on post. The signs read, "No liquor, no cameras, and no guns."

J. A. Terteling and Sons, along with army engineers, began building the base at the end of November 1942. While very few photographs exist of Mountain Home Army Air Base being constructed, this shot clearly shows workers pouring asphalt onto the taxiways. In the background are three of the four hangars built to house the B-24 Liberators. These hangars still exist today.

Workmen grade the ground in preparation for the concrete being poured. While not evident in this photograph, the majority of the construction took place in the winter months of 1942 and early 1943. To thaw the ground, the Tertelings mixed 6,500 pounds of salt with water to create a solution that they poured onto the hardened soil. The runway officially opened on August 7, 1943.

Col. Arthur J. Melanson had the honor of being Mountain Home's second commander and is known by many as the father of Mountain Home Army Air Field. He had served with the U.S. Army Air Corps since November 1917 and had an interesting career as a flyer, serving not only in the United States but also in the Philippines. While Melanson was commander of Gowen Field from 1940 to 1942, the 2nd Air Force noted that the Boise outpost was a model base in construction and administrative procedures. Because of this, the 2nd Air Force commander requested that Colonel Melanson transfer to Mountain Home so that the Army Air Forces could take advantage of his exceptional ability in organizing new air bases. After he oversaw the construction of the base, he personally accompanied Gen. Eugene L. Eubank on a tour of the post. General Eubank, the director of bombardment in charge of training and supervision of the entire Army Air Forces, expressed himself as being very pleased with the base and the job Mountain Home had done in preparing aircrews for combat.

The master of ceremonies, O. C. Marler, prepares to sing the national anthem in a formal procedure awarding the Army-Navy E mark of distinction to J. A. Terteling and Sons. Below, the ladies wearing their V for Victory bonnets wait to sell war stamps. The war savings stamp was a patriotic program used by the U.S. Treasury to help fund participation in World Wars I and II. Principally aimed at school-aged children, the stamps were available in 10¢, 25¢, 50¢, $1, and $5 denominations.

Gen. Warren T. Hannum of the Salt Lake City–Pacific Division of the U.S. Army Corps of Engineers addresses the assembly. Col. Hugo Rush is seated to his right wearing sunglasses. In the general's speech, he said "the Army-Navy production award stands as our fighting forces joint recognition of exceptional performance on the production and construction front and for the determined, persevering, unbeatable spirit which can be satisfied only by achieving today what yesterday seemed impossible."

From left to right, Gov. C. A. Bottolfsen, Gen. Warren T. Hannum, Vady Jane Terteling, Joseph W. Terteling, and Nixon Terteling pose for a photograph during the Army-Navy E Award ceremony. The governor's opening speech recognized the efforts of the Terteling Company, terming the base "a patriotic inspiration to all of us in Idaho, to labor, to industry and to the general public." Prior to this photograph, Col. Hugo P. Rush spoke. As the commander of the 15th Wing and chief of staff of the 2nd Bomber Command, both located at Gowen Field and both in charge of the training at Mountain Home, he accepted the base on behalf of General Eubank. In his acceptance speech, he stated that "he doubted if there was another airfield in the world that had three runways as fine as Mountain Home's. He went on to add that each runway stretched out for two miles and could support a 60,000-pound airplane landing at 100 miles per hour."

Vandy Jane Terteling proudly grasps the coveted "E" flag displayed by her sons, Joseph and Noel Terteling. To the far right, employee representative Hugo Trelick also lends a hand with the huge pennant.

Mountain Home's three-man color guard, Sergeants Nisser, Brown, and Vorrel, hoisted the large red and blue "E" pennant to the top of the staff. Prior to this, Lt. G. A. Hebert, the officer in charge of navy recruiting in Idaho, presented "E" lapel pins to the company's employees, who were represented by Hugo Trelick.

This aerial view shows a Mountain Home B-24D being flown by a crew from the 470th Bombardment Group. While the B-24 did not receive nearly as much media attention as its B-17 sister, more Liberators were built than any other airplane during World War II.

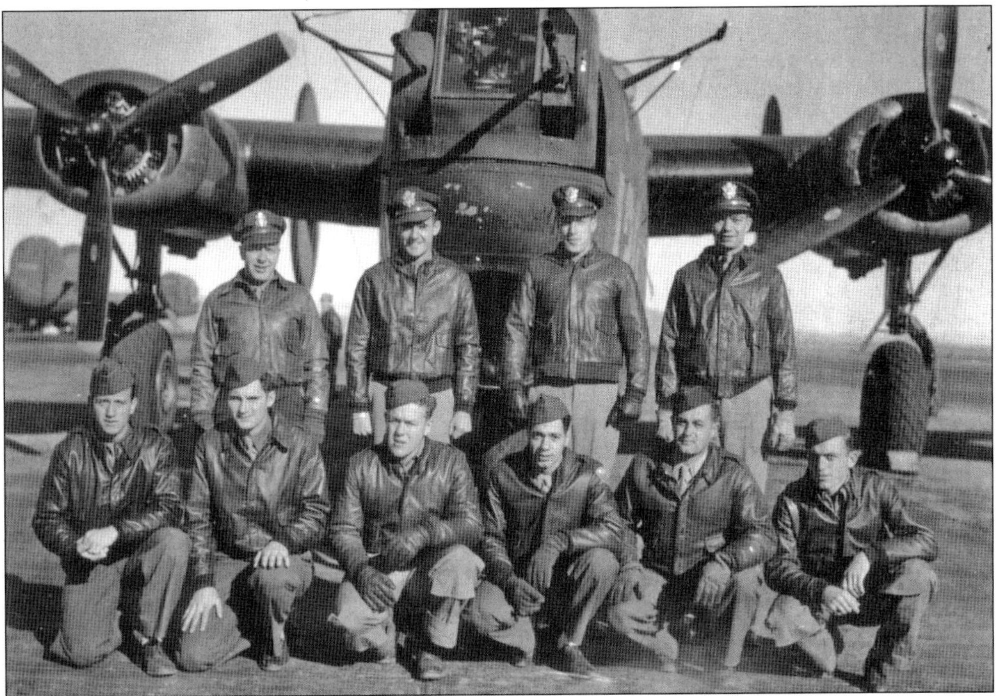

Crew 207 of the 470th Bombardment Group stands in front of its B-24D, which has been modified with a tail turret placed in its nose. Most B-24Ds had the old greenhouse nose, as seen in the photograph above. The added machine guns in the front made the aircraft much more survivable in a head on attack. From left to right are (first row) Sergeants J. M. Close, C. E. Faulhaber, J. B. Cook, M. J. De Brino, R. G. Thompson, and C. C. Lindey; (second row) Second Lieutenants R. H. Tagerman, W. F. Sullivan, J. M. Buckey, and J. Brenneman.

This aerial view of Mountain Home was taken in July 1943 and shows just how sparse the surrounding area was. Of particular note is the lack of buildings on the base. At this point in Mountain Home's evolution, its structures consisted mainly of tar paper shacks with very few fully finished facilities. It was, to say the least, bare bones.

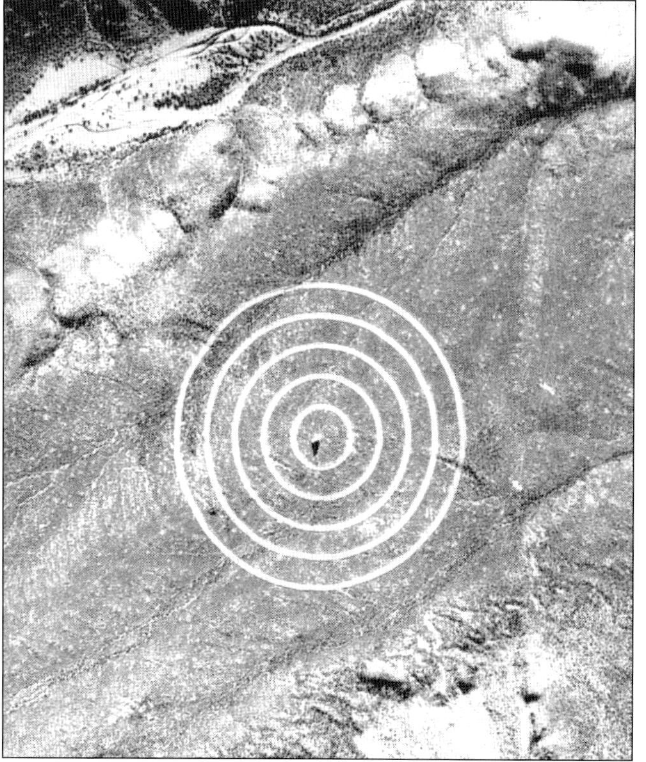

The Army Air Forces utilized the airspace throughout Idaho for gunnery training but cordoned off specific areas for bombing. To do this, the U.S. Army Corps of Engineers built multiple precision bombing rings in several out-of-the-way areas. Eventually the base would open Saylor Creek Bombing Range, but for the meantime, these rings filled the bill. In this view, a bombardier has released his ordnance, and he has snapped a photograph of the bomb landing dead center in the concentric ring. The aircrews called this a shack.

Although many of the buildings had a facade made of tar paper, Colonel Melanson's building had the amenities suited to a man of his rank. Not only did he have lap siding, his building also contained three potbellied stoves.

Contrasting with the base commander's building, the 470th Bombardment Group Headquarters consisted of tar paper held down with skinny pieces of wood. While the tar paper kept the water out, in the summer, the sand and wind invaded every nook and cranny of the building. Although the building did not have lap siding, it did have a very decorative emblem.

During World War II, instrument-flying training became all-important, as long-range aircraft like bombers were introduced. To develop coordinated training of aircraft crews, the military requested that Edwin Link adapt his instrument flight simulator for celestial navigational training. Mountain Home housed four of these trainers in structures that looked similar to grain towers with eight sides.

The trainer was housed in an air-conditioned, eight-walled building with aircrew members positioned in a fuselage similar to the Link Trainer. The fuselage carried a pilot, navigator, bombardier, and radioman. A synthetic night sky was lit for celestial navigation while ground features were projected on a white screen beneath the fuselage. The pilot would fly the aircraft while the navigator used sky or ground references to reach an objective, where the bombardier would take over to complete the mission. The simulator instructor could introduce bumpy flying conditions, changes of wind, create daylight or nightfall, scurry clouds across the sky, or arrange static to confuse the radioman.

Due to the location of the base, wildlife tended to wander into the living and work areas. Wayne Stinson took it upon himself to befriend this badger and make it his unit's mascot. After his commanding officer found that Stinson had captured a wild animal, he was quickly ordered to release the beast.

While waiting for transport from the Mountain Home depot, Wayne Stinson and a few friends dressed a local child in a gas mask and posed for a quick photograph.

Because of Gowen Field's proximity to Mountain Home, the two bases often shared equipment. Here gunners practice shooting skeet in the open desert of Idaho. This contraption simulated the top turret on a B-24.

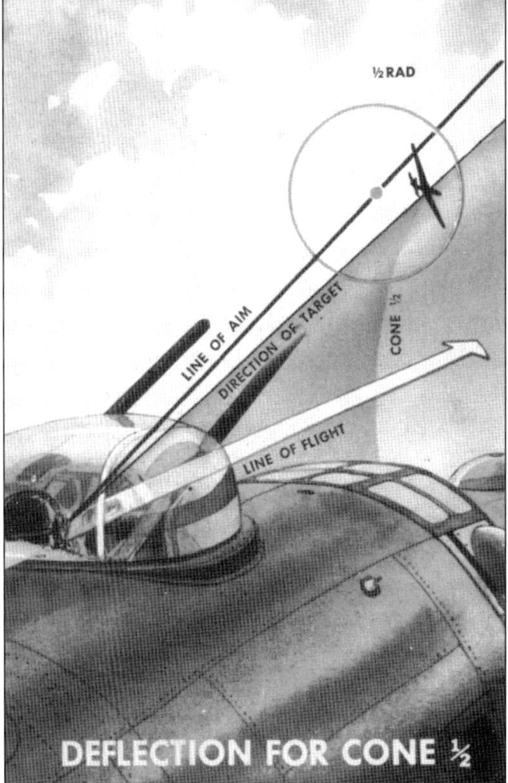

Each member of the aircrew became familiar with how to fire the machine guns and how to accurately lead an enemy aircraft to destruction. Here in an excerpt from "Get that Fighter," the illustration clearly shows how much a gunner would need to lead the enemy in a straight and level flight path. If the aircraft was banking or jinking flak, the job became much more difficult.

Besides training aircrews, the instructors at Mountain Home and Gowen Field also schooled their students on the proper use of small arms. Here a lieutenant coaches an enlisted man on the proper procedures for firing an M-1 Garand.

Here is another good shot of a 470th Bomb Group aircrew. These 10 men look as if they are having a good day in the blustery Idaho weather. The 470th arrived at Mountain Home in August 1943 and departed in January 1944. Once they left, the 20th Base Headquarters Squadron assumed the duties of training B-24 aircrews for war.

In the immediate aftermath of Pearl Harbor, the military needed complete flying units for the war, but by the end of 1943, this capability had nearly been filled. In November 1943, the 20th Base Headquarters Squadron, consisting of just over 100 men, arrived at Mountain Home and began a replacement training program to backfill the aircrews that had been lost in battle. This was the mission of Mountain Home until the end of the war.

Here the 470th Bombardment Group, with its subordinate squadrons, falls into formation for a parade during a base open house. Mountain Home opened its gates to the public to educate them on the mission at Mountain Home as well as an act of good stewardship.

On August 1, 1944, Mountain Home Army Air Field opened its gates and invited the public to view the base. In a word of welcome, the station commander, Lt. Col. Clarence D. Barhill, expressed, "On this 37th anniversary of the establishment of the Army Air Forces and the 35th anniversary of the first military airplane, we of the Mountain Home Army Air Filed, welcome the chance to show the people of Mountain Home and Elmore County this field, because, although it is ours at present, the field really belongs to you."

This rough map showed the layout of the base in 1944. It consisted of a few boulevards, with the main routes that ran north and south labeled as A and B Streets. The commander, Lt. Col. Clarence Barnhill, opened most of the base to the public with exception of zones where aircrews trained for live missions.

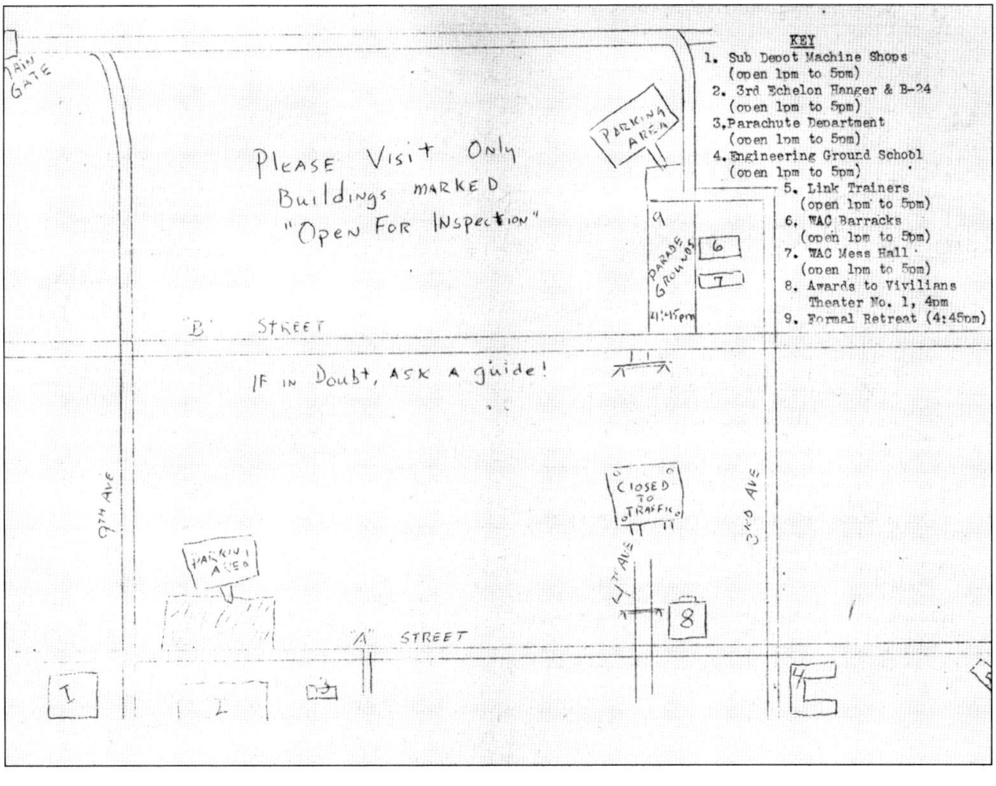

MAIN GATE
PARKING AREA
Please Visit Only Buildings marked "Open For Inspection"
PARADE GROUNDS
4:45pm
'B' STREET
IF IN Doubt, ASK A guide!
9TH AVE
CLOSED TO TRAFFIC
3RD AVE
PARKING AREA
'A' STREET

KEY
1. Sub Depot Machine Shops (open 1pm to 5pm)
2. 3rd Echelon Hanger & B-24 (open 1pm to 5pm)
3. Parachute Department (open 1pm to 5pm)
4. Engineering Ground School (open 1pm to 5pm)
5. Link Trainers (open 1pm to 5pm)
6. WAC Barracks (open 1pm to 5pm)
7. WAC Mess Hall (open 1pm to 5pm)
8. Awards to Vivilians Theater No. 1, 4pm
9. Formal Retreat (4:45pm)

This spidery-looking contraption was officially known as the A-2 bombing trainer but was better known as the "bug chaser." Used in a hangar, the trainer simulated the principle features of an actual bombing mission. It had two purposes: to help the bombardier learn how to operate the sight and to help him learn the procedure he would use in the air.

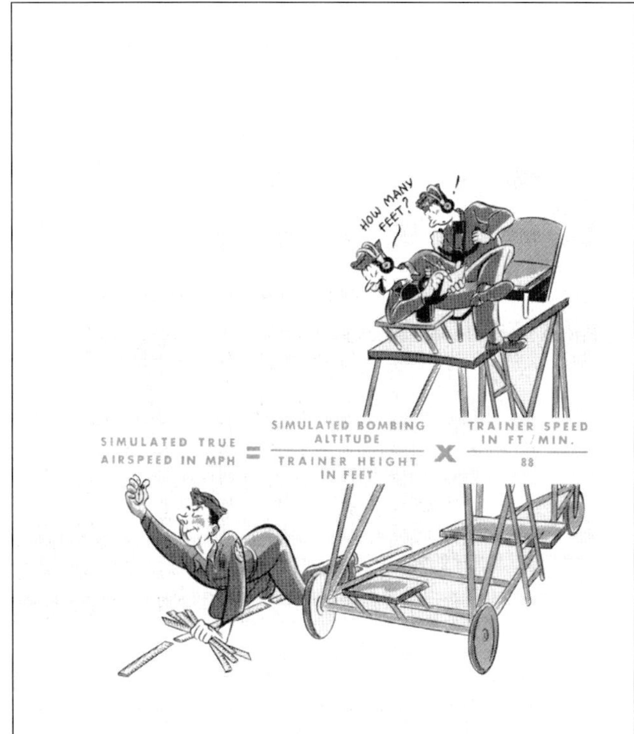

This cartoon from the student bombing manual poked fun at the math needed to compute the simulated true airspeed in miles per hour. The data needed for the algebraic formula was manually measured, then computed by hand. While this trainer was a valuable piece of equipment, it was subordinate to the realistic training achieved over the Idaho ranges.

Colonel Melanson encouraged his men to get out and see Idaho. While the leadership held activities on base, many GIs traveled to Boise and Gowen Field, while others tried their hand at local attractions. This group of 2nd Air Force men, with one lovely lady, opted for a cooler sport: skiing. While the author is not positive of the Idaho location, it is more than likely Sun Valley.

It was very common for men from Gowen Field or Mountain Home to travel to each base and participate in the local festivities. This included dances and parties, but on special occasions, a band other than the Gowen Field orchestra would pass through Idaho. Here the Del Courtney Orchestra of big band fame prepares to entertain troops from both Gowen and Mountain Home.

In December 1943, Colonel Melanson departed Mountain Home, and Lt. Col. Clarence D. Barnhill assumed command. The 2nd Air Force charged Colonel Barnhill with overseeing Mountain Home as it trained two bombardment groups for combat.

The 490th Bombardment Group arrived at Mountain Home in December 1943 and departed for the European theater the following April. Shown here is an aircrew from that unit. From left to right are (first row) Staff Sergeant Bob Purdy (Sperry ball turret gunner), Staff Sergeant Ed Luchun (top turret gunner), Staff Sergeant Chester Koziol (nose turret gunner), Staff Sergeant Ed Moreno (tail gunner), Technical Sergeant Ed Guriren (engineer); (second row) 2nd Lt. Virgil Renfro (bombardier), 2nd Lt. Al Guilio (copilot), 2nd Lt. Al Hall (navigator), and Staff Sergeant Ed Folts (radio operator).

In this photograph, a formation of B-24s flies over the Snake River. Shown in July 1943, the river looks cool and refreshing from this altitude. In just a few short months, the water would be frigid and frozen. Today this same shot is often recreated using the 366th Fighter Wing's aircraft, but boaters can be seen floating down the river.

From this operations room, aircrews and administrative personnel could track the group's aircraft. On the boards, the enlisted men chalked in the name of the B-24 pilot, his aircraft tail number, when he departed the base, and his projected return time.

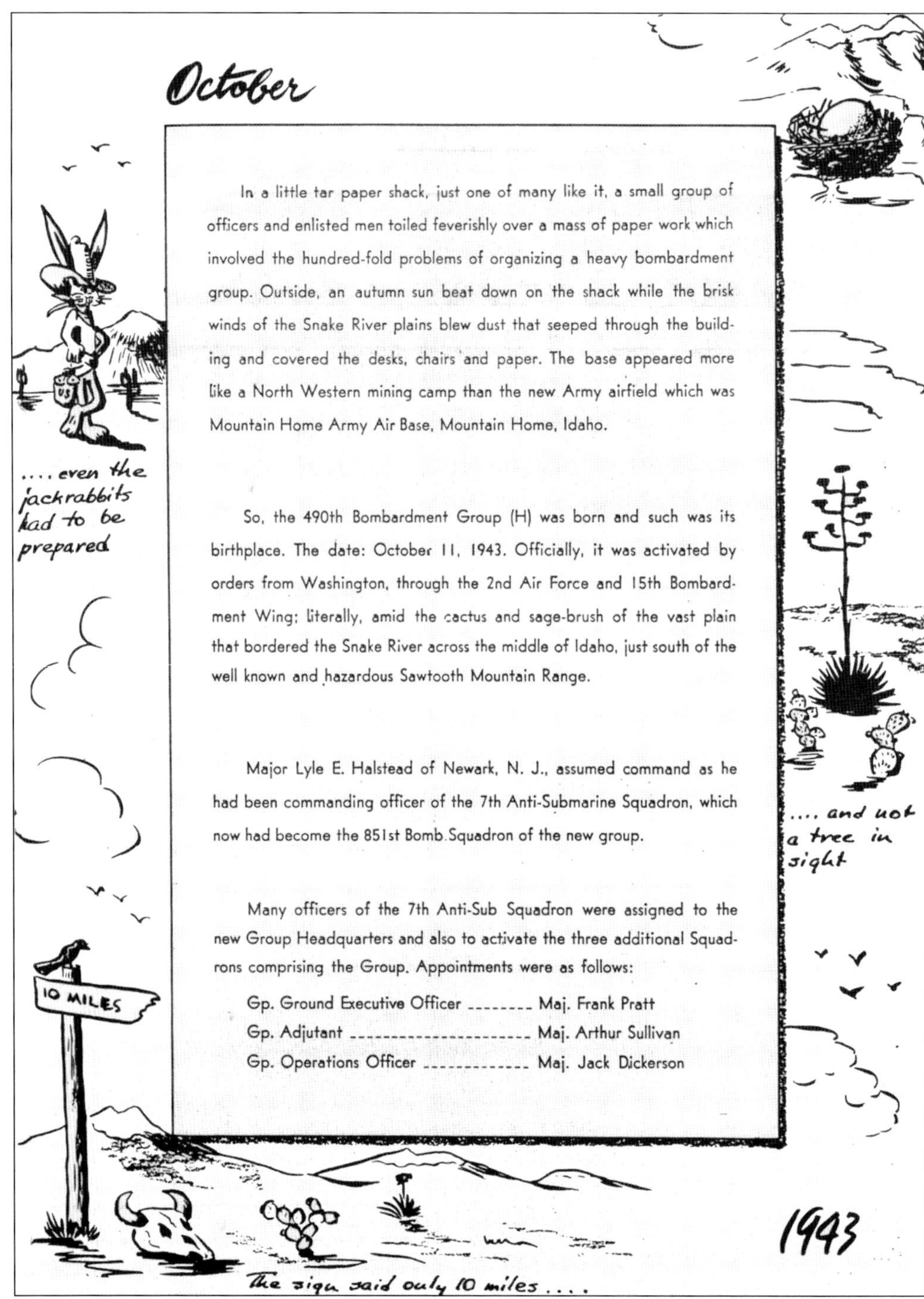

October

In a little tar paper shack, just one of many like it, a small group of officers and enlisted men toiled feverishly over a mass of paper work which involved the hundred-fold problems of organizing a heavy bombardment group. Outside, an autumn sun beat down on the shack while the brisk winds of the Snake River plains blew dust that seeped through the building and covered the desks, chairs and paper. The base appeared more like a North Western mining camp than the new Army airfield which was Mountain Home Army Air Base, Mountain Home, Idaho.

So, the 490th Bombardment Group (H) was born and such was its birthplace. The date: October 11, 1943. Officially, it was activated by orders from Washington, through the 2nd Air Force and 15th Bombardment Wing; literally, amid the cactus and sage-brush of the vast plain that bordered the Snake River across the middle of Idaho, just south of the well known and hazardous Sawtooth Mountain Range.

Major Lyle E. Halstead of Newark, N. J., assumed command as he had been commanding officer of the 7th Anti-Submarine Squadron, which now had become the 851st Bomb. Squadron of the new group.

Many officers of the 7th Anti-Sub Squadron were assigned to the new Group Headquarters and also to activate the three additional Squadrons comprising the Group. Appointments were as follows:

Gp. Ground Executive Officer .... Maj. Frank Pratt
Gp. Adjutant .... Maj. Arthur Sullivan
Gp. Operations Officer .... Maj. Jack Dickerson

Shortly after World War II ended, Technical Sergeant Frederick R. Holland and Lt. Col. Lawrence S. Lightner compiled a short history of the 490th Bombardment Group. In this excerpt, the two men describe Mountain Home Army Air Field as it appeared in October 1943. In that early time, the group had not officially formed, and the men who wrote this stood by in casual status waiting for their B-24s to arrive.

The 490th Bomb Group was made up of four bomb squadrons (848th, 849th, 850th, and the 851st), with each having the respective aircraft disciplines to complete daily missions. Here a portion of the 851st Ordnance Company poses for a photograph. These men were responsible for the construction of bombs and the accountability of ammunition.

In April 1944, the 490th Bomb Group departed Mountain Home headed for Eye, East Anglia, England. From there the crews deployed their B-24s, delivering devastation to the German Army. In this photograph, B-24 Liberator crews bomb oil refineries at Misburg, Germany.

This was the first post exchange (PX) at Mountain Home. While it looked dreary, the items it contained kept the residents of the dusty airbase very happy. The exchange system began in the late 1800s, but it really got under way during World War I. The first documented use of the term PX is found in a book of exchange council meetings at Fort McKinley, Philippines. Up until that point, the military generally referred to exchanges as canteens. Eventually the PX moved into a better facility, and this was used as a tavern.

These enlisted men anxiously wait to purchase candy or stationery. Prior to World War II beginning, the Army Exchange Service (AES) went into operation. As the war moved overseas, so did AES; its employees quickly adopted the motto "We go where you go." For young men and women far away from family, the PX reminded them of home. In the 1950s, AES reorganized and is now widely recognized as the Army and Air Force Exchange Service (AAFES).

The residents of Mountain Home had very few choices of where to eat, but most preferred the PX cafeteria. Here a lady offers a milkshake to a B-24 aircrew member while a corporal looks on.

The other option for a bellyful of food was one of the base mess halls. Here members of the 801st Bomb Squadron pose for a quick photograph. In the background, the cook peeks through from the kitchen.

On September 3, 1943, the base chapel opened its doors for its first service. With its opening, the base chaplain made arrangements to have as many events as possible, including Catholic, Protestant, and Jewish services. He also made arrangements for the establishment of a chapel choir and a service of recorded classical and semiclassical music.

Here the base chapel has been dressed accordingly, and a mass is being held. Through the special service bulletin produced every week, base personnel learned of service times and special events. Due to the remoteness of Mountain Home, leadership made great efforts to entertain the men by introducing sports. This built their physical bodies, while the church tended to their spirits.

This photograph, taken by Cpl. Wayne Stinson, shows a typical enlisted men's barracks during World War II. Those who were lucky enough to garner a bunk near the potbellied stove stayed warm during the winter, while the others threw an additional wool blanket on their beds.

Sgt. Loyal E. Carnahan, from the 802nd Intelligence Office, painted this mural on the squadron briefing room wall. It shows B-24s bombing entrenched enemy troops on some distant tropical island. Murals like this one were very common at Mountain Home during the war. They lifted morale, and the blank walls gave those fledgling artists a canvas to paint on.

213th Combat Crew Training Station
Mountain Home Air Field
Mountain Home, Idaho

This is to Certify, That

2ND LT ROBERT L. BARBOUR 02071513

has satisfactorily completed the course
of training for combat crews
as prescribed by Headquarters, Second Air Force
and given at

Mountain Home Army Air Field, Idaho

Given on this 11TH day of DECEMBER in the year of Our Lord, one thousand, nine hundred and forty-four.

Attest:

John T. Compton
Major, Air Corps
Director of Training

Colonel, Air Corps
Commanding

In March 1944, the 213th Base Unit took over the responsibilities of training aircrews at Mountain Home and also braced for a slight mission change. The Army Air Forces no longer needed full squadrons or groups to deploy, but rather needed replacement crews for airmen lost in overseas battles. In May 1944, training personnel from Peterson Field, Colorado, arrived to establish the program. This is a certificate issued to 2nd Lt. Robert D. Barbour, of Boise, Idaho, when he successfully completed his training at Mountain Home.

A B-24 sits on the ramp as the sun sets.

On June 15, 1943, the 2nd Air Force activated the 823rd Women's Auxiliary Air Corps (WAACs) at Mountain Home. These ladies took over many of the duties that had been performed by men, including administration, Link Trainer instruction, radio mechanic, sheet-metal working, weather observing, and many other disciplines within the Army Air Forces. Their sister unit, the WASPs, flew the 494th Bombardment Group's B-24s from the factory to Mountain Home in April 1944.

This corporal is not looking too happy for this photograph. These two men held administrative typing jobs documenting training and supply.

Mountain Home Army Air Field

MOUNTAIN HOME, IDAHO

426TH ARMY AIR FORCES, BASE UNIT
COMBAT CREW TRAINING STATION, (HEAVY)

ARMY AIR FIELD

Mountain Home, Idaho

In February 1945, the base underwent yet another change, as the 426th Base Unit took over responsibility for training. This is the cover from a graduation pamphlet for Mountain Home class 3-26-1945.

Combat crew 351-5 had their photograph taken in May 1945, prior to graduation. From left to right are gunner Steven G. Bryan (Iowa), copilot Alan M. Owen (Kentucky), pilot Robert O. Phillips (Texas), navigator William M. Harrelson (Arkansas), and engineer William J. Naylor (Kansas).

The Sage

Vol. 1, No. 8 | ARMY AIR BASE, MOUNTAIN HOME, IDAHO. | Aug. 12, 1943

Colors Presented to 470th Bomb Group

The first edition of the *Sage* appeared on May 26, 1943, and ran until March 4, 1944. In this August 12 edition, the weekly announced the 470th's arrival to the base. The Boise Statesman Printing Company donated the photographs and printing to increase morale. Due to the shortage of help during 1944, the firm could not longer produce the newspaper.

The three air police leading the parade are from the 5th Air Police Squadron at Mountain Home Air Force Base. This photograph was taken in 1949 during an air force appreciation event in downtown Mountain Home. Since that time, the parade has become an annual tradition but has transformed into a two-day party with bands, food, and lots of socializing.

A B-24D lifts off for a practice mission over Idaho. As the war came to a close, Mountain Home's fate was unknown. For a brief period, there was talk of placing B-32 Dominators at the field, but that quickly evaporated. The last B-24 left Mountain Home in September 1945.

After the base had been closed for several years, the 5th Reconnaissance Group arrived in May 1949 and began operating its RB-17s. While wearing heavy overcoats, these men pose for a picture in the winter of 1949. While there was no snow in this photograph, the average temperature hovered between 22 and 38 degrees, with the wind incessantly gusting up to 24 knots. Of interesting note, in 1949, the area only received snow in the month of June.

Two

The Cold War Heats Up

After being closed almost two years, in April 1951, the ultra-secret Air Resupply and Communications (ARC) wings reopened Mountain Home. The unit did little to alter the infrastructure of the base, as is evident in this photograph of the main gate. Several years later, Strategic Air Command assigned the 9th Bomb Wing to the base; over a decade, the 9th breathed life into the desolate station. This photograph was taken in late 1953, before the new gate had been designed and constructed. As with the gate during World War II, the military police posted instructions for entry. The sign reads, "Drivers declare all unauthorized passengers to the main gate guard."

In February 1951, the air force activated the Air Resupply and Communications Service after a request from an agency outside of the Department of Defense. The CIA called for a service similar to that conducted by the Carpetbagger units of World War II. As part of the aerial resupply mission, the ARC units would introduce ranger-type personnel behind enemy lines and provide supplies. To do this, they needed an aircraft with a 4,000-nautical-mile range. The only aircraft available was the B-29.

To introduce the ranger-type personnel deep into Soviet-occupied areas, the ACR units needed the B-29. They pulled a number of these airplanes from mothballs at Robins AFB, Georgia, and restored the birds to duty. For the mission, the mechanics removed all guns less the tail gun and cut a "joe hole" where the aft belly gun turret had been. The rangers would drop through this hole while their supplies hung like melons in the bomb bays.

The ARC units used the World War II infrastructure and made little to no modifications. They saw Mountain Home as just a waypoint to their final destination. In this view, two B-29s sit in front of Hangar 211.

To insert and extract personnel, the ARC units used the SA-16 Albatross. They painted these aircraft black so to not be seen at night. They practiced their covert missions in the skies over Mountain Home, Boise, and northern Nevada.

This is a view of the Snake River 10 years after the trio of B-24s flew past. See page 29.

This is a sunset shot of Mountain Home's base operations in 1952. Of note, a C-119 Boxcar is visible to the far right. The ARC units used the Boxcar for missions that did not require the 4,000-mile combat radius of the B-29. They operated this airplane to deliver cargo and troops behind enemy lines.

The ARC units did little to nothing to improve the base. Personnel continued to live in the World War II barracks, with their tar papered walls and potbellied stoves.

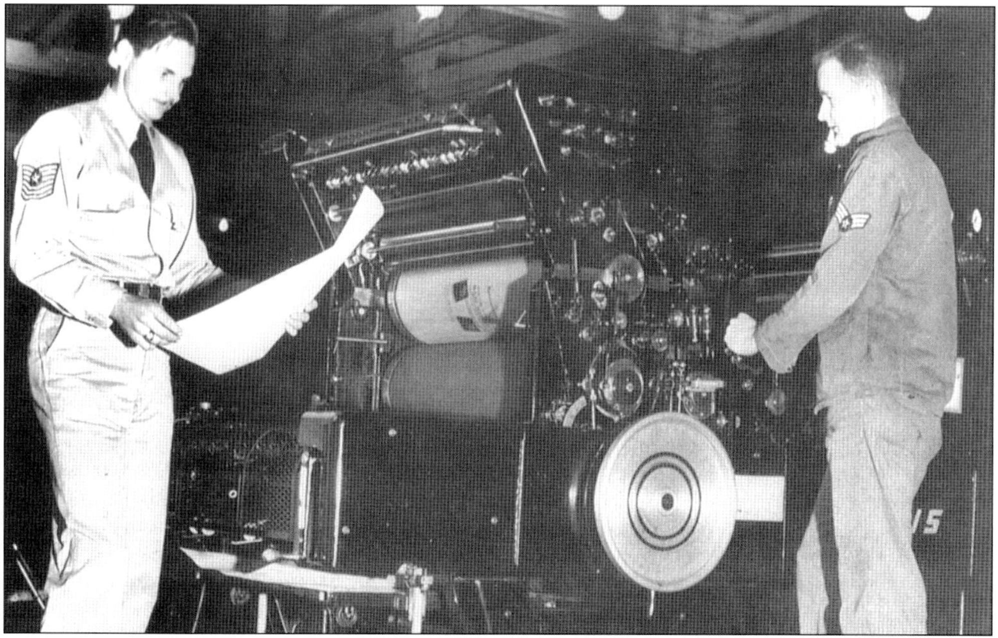

A master sergeant and a buck sergeant check the clarity of a psychological leaflet being made on a printing press. The ARC's second mission was to conduct psychological warfare on the enemy by dropping leaflets and blasting audio from orbiting aircraft. The leaflets were conceived and designed by a talented pool of ARC psychological warfare (psywar) officers trained at Georgetown University's Institute of Languages and Linguistics in Washington, D.C.

The 581st ARC Wing left Mountain Home in June 1952 and eventually conducted operations in Korea. Its psywar unit designed and dropped many leaflets on the North Korean Army. This leaflet depicts Joseph Stalin as a puppet master to the North Korean leader Kim II Sung.

The reverse side has a conversation between Stalin and Kim. Written in Korean, the leaflet more than likely states that the North Korean president knows that his troops are suffering, but he does not care. It was the perfect form of psychological warfare and worked very well to demoralize the enemy.

The 1300th Food Services intramural basketball team is, from left to right, (first row) Shimight James (3), Robert Davis (12), Brent Gambill (5), and Isaac Rivera (4); (second row) Chuck Deloach (11), Thomas Hackett (10), Robert Knatzschman (20), Gene Mullins (14), Adolph Cranford (15), and Gerald Phillips (13).

In November 1951, the air force activated the 1300th Air Base Wing as the host unit at Mountain Home AFB. The subordinate units ran the various operations around the base, including the mess facilities. This photograph shows the men of the 1300th Food Services Squadron in Chow Hall 2. Chuck Deloach, a Mountain Home resident, is sitting in the first row on the very right.

Shown is the emblem of the 9th Bomb Wing. The shield, with green and black sections, represents the colors of the old Air Service Corps. The silver represents the Rio Grande, symbolic of Texas City, Texas, in 1913. The rattlesnake on the top part of the shield represents the wing's part in the Mexican Expedition of 1916. The gold band and four crosses represent the wing's action in World War I. *Semper paratus* translates as "Always Ready."

The 9th Bomb Wing arrived at Mountain Home in May 1953 on the heels of the ARC units. In the beginning, the unit operated the B-29 bomber and the KB-29 refueler. Here the long hoses that pass gas to waiting airplanes string behind the refueler.

Eventually the 9th Bomb Wing upgraded to the newest bomber of the time, the B-47 Stratojet. At the same time, the unit abandoned its KB-29 refuelers and began operating the KC-97 Stratotanker.

In this snapshot, the photographer is looking down through the refueling window as the KC-97 boom operator refuels a B-47 bomber. Note the exhaust coming from the tanker's engines.

This crew of a new KC-97 is happy to have their photograph taken, and they are even happier to be part of the SAC team. The Boeing KC-97 was the refueling tanker version of the C-97 Stratofreighter, a 74-ton, multipurpose airplane combining both transport and aerial refueling tanker capabilities. In 1942, Boeing began development of a freight-carrying airplane able to match the B-29 in speed, range, and ruggedness. They utilized a number of the B-29's components, including wings, empennage, engines, and landing gear. The diameter of the B-29 fuselage, however, was not large enough for the proposed missions. Boeing engineers met the challenge with what became known as the double-bubble cross section. The lower section retained the B-29 fuselage—with cargo compartments instead of bomb bays—while the 11-foot-wide upper section boasted huge rear "clamshell" loading doors. The resulting 6,140 cubic feet of usable cargo space was more than double the volume of any other transport at the time.

Although the 9th Bomb Wing received ultramodern airplanes for its mission, life at Mountain Home AFB remained very primitive. As seen in this photograph, the attacking tumbleweeds had to be rounded up on a frequent basis and put back out to pasture. In reality, after gathering these menaces, the men dropped them in a ditch, doused them with gas, and set them ablaze. This still occurs today.

Shortly one year after the 9th Bomber Wing's arrival at Mountain Home AFB, it began a program to refurbish the base. This included new buildings and upgrades to existing facilities. A worker tears the tar paper from one of the World War II buildings and prepares it for a face-lift. Some of these structures would continue to survive long into the 1980s.

By 1954, a plan was well under way to tear down the old World War II buildings and begin construction of new modern facilities. Nonetheless, the base gate remained unchanged by this time. Note that these air police have begun to wear the uniform of the U.S. Air Force rather than the U.S. Army's attire.

As with the front gate, the base continued to use the World War II visitors' center up until the mid-1950s. Eventually the 9th Bomb Wing would replace the main gate and visitors' center with a contemporary-looking building acceptable for a wing operating the modern B-47.

Due to the nature of the B-47's mission, many aspects of the job had to be kept under wraps. In Building 216, the 9th housed the Special Weapons School, where B-47 aircrews polished their skills on how to deliver a nuclear weapon. For this reason, this building, as well as many other structures on Mountain Home AFB, had very restricted access.

Building 224, the target intelligence training facility, housed the equipment and materials needed to educate young airmen in the intricate details of how to target the enemy's most vital areas. Again, due to the nature of the materials present, this building was very restricted. Note the barbwire fence.

Throughout the 1950s and 1960s, the base library took shelter in a World War II facility but served its patrons very well. Today the library is housed in the former NCO club.

This young "one-striper" mans the front desk of the base library. With the cutbacks in personnel, the majority of these positions have been outsourced to contractors. Where the base library of the 1950s only offered books and magazines, the library of today has computer access along with a good selection of movies.

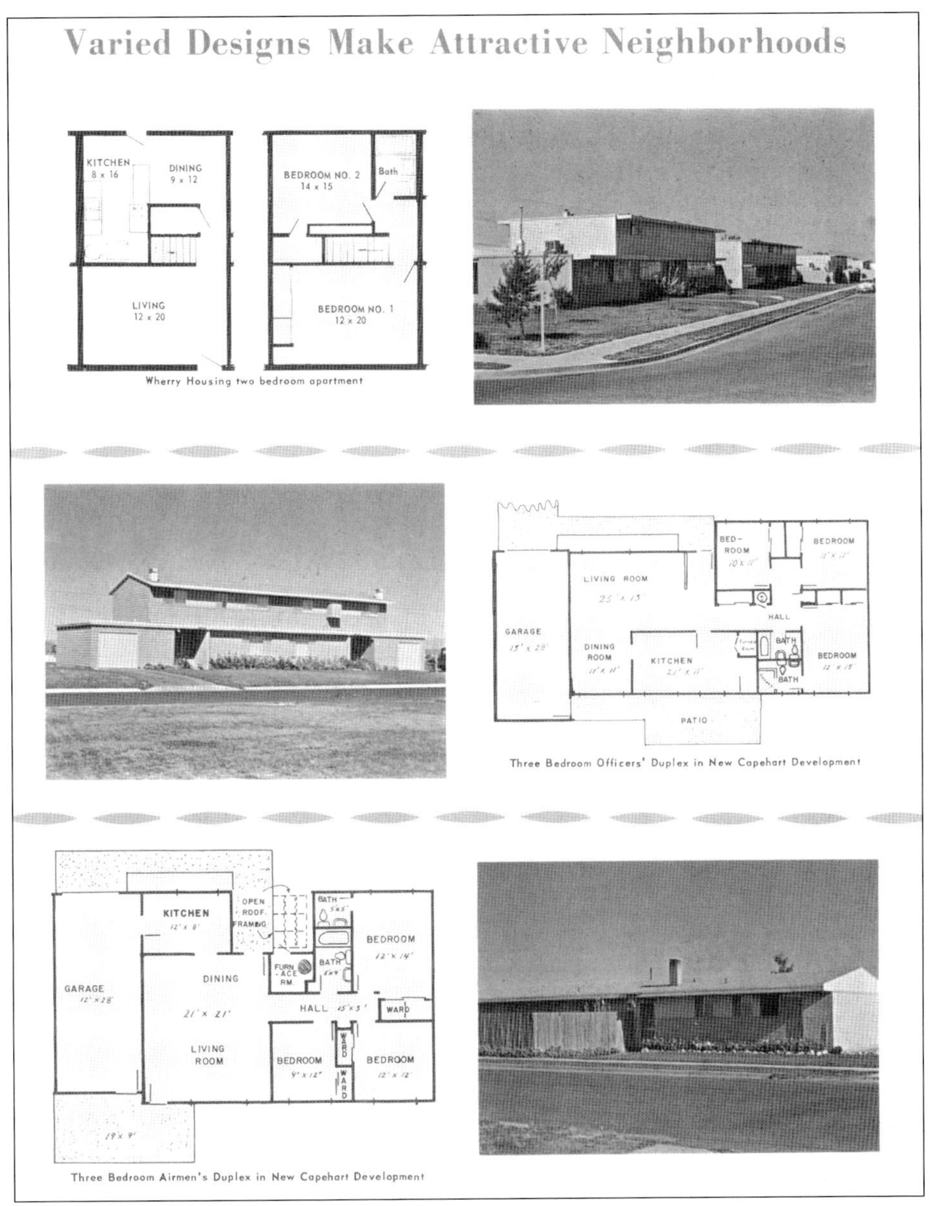

In August 1949, the Senate passed the Wherry Housing Act, a program sponsored by Sen. Kenneth Wherry of Nebraska. This bill allowed private developers to build housing on government-owned land. With the ARC units not making many upgrades to the base, new housing construction did not begin until August 1954, after the 9th Bomb Wing had arrived. The air force awarded the Centex Construction Corporation of Dallas, Texas, a $5-million contract to build 500 units that included central heating, individual garages, concrete patios enclosed by protective fences, electric ranges, refrigerators, and hot-water heaters. Furthermore, they built a fenced playing area complete with slides, swings, and other playground equipment. The rentals ran according to the size of the units, with airmen's apartments costing $50 for one bedroom, $60 for two bedrooms, and $70 for three bedrooms. The air force charged officers an additional $10 per month for each type of apartment. This photograph shows the layouts for the three types of housing built at Mountain Home AFB during the 1950s and 1960s.

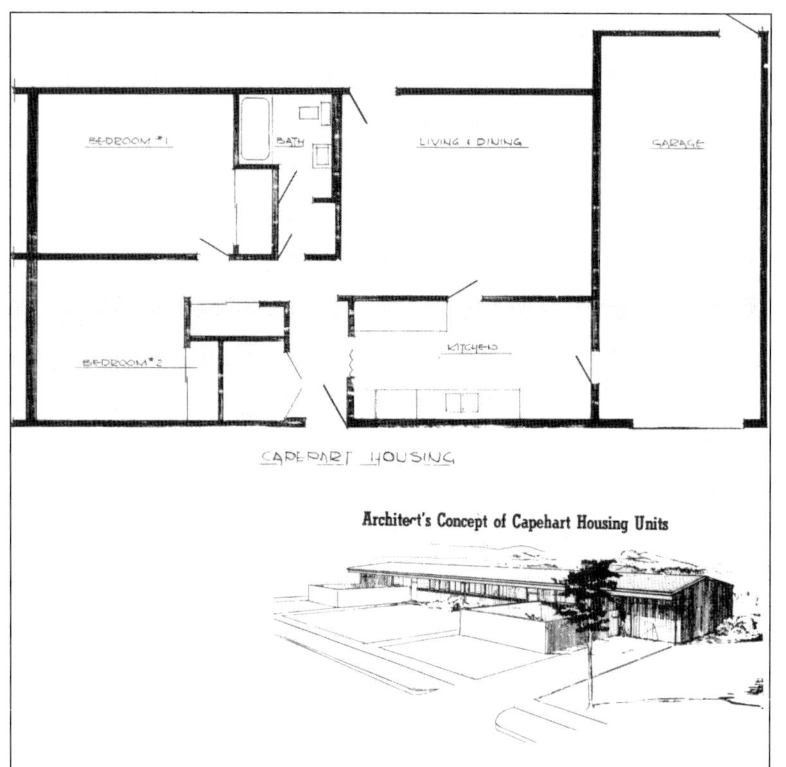

Between 1956 and 1962, the military witnessed roughly 115,000 houses built under this program. At Mountain Home, the Army Corps of Engineers constructed the Woodland Groves, Gunfighter Manor, and Presidential Acres subdivisions as Capehart houses.

What was originally known as the Shell Housing was built after World War II; the first permanent structures on base. Base personnel referred to the units as Shell Housing because the outside was permanent, while the insides could be quickly altered. Due to the lack of housing in the 1950s, base engineers remodeled the interior, where four families could reside in each shell. After the Wherry and Capehart programs relieved the lack of housing, the base remodeled these units for the base commander and his immediate staff.

Four years after the Wherry housing program began on base, Idaho's governor Robert E. Smylie broke ground for the new Capehart housing development. The construction called for 860 units and began in December 1958. As planned, the military would take control of the units by December 1959, but weather delays forced the program out until 1962. Here the winter weather has halted all construction in January 1962.

New water lines and power lines needed to be run in order to accommodate all of the new building on base. Workers drill holes and place new power poles up and down B Street.

Along with the new housing and work facilities, base engineers also oversaw the construction to support the B-47 operations. Here workers build one of three fuel storage tanks.

The wing had no way of directly fueling the B-47, so it used trucks to move the gas to the flight line. This photograph shows the vehicle storage yard. Because of the B-47's size and its appetite for fuel, it took the transportation squadron several trips to fill the aircraft.

While this nondescript photograph tells very little about the base exchange (BX), the text that accompanied the picture was priceless. The base received over $2 million for an extensive building campaign, which included a new BX. Once completed, the beer bar would be moved to occupy a portion of the BX, which was stocked with clothing. This section would be used to handle the overflow "coffee" crowds when the beer bar was closed.

On Sunday, December 5, 1954, the 9th Bomb Wing commander, Col. William C. Kingsbury, cut the ribbon hanging across the altar, officially opening the chapel. Rev. Hartzell Cobbs, pastor of the First Christian Church in Boise, gave the dedication message and Airman Second Class George Hahn sang "Bless this House." This chapel still stands today, while the churches built during World War II have been moved.

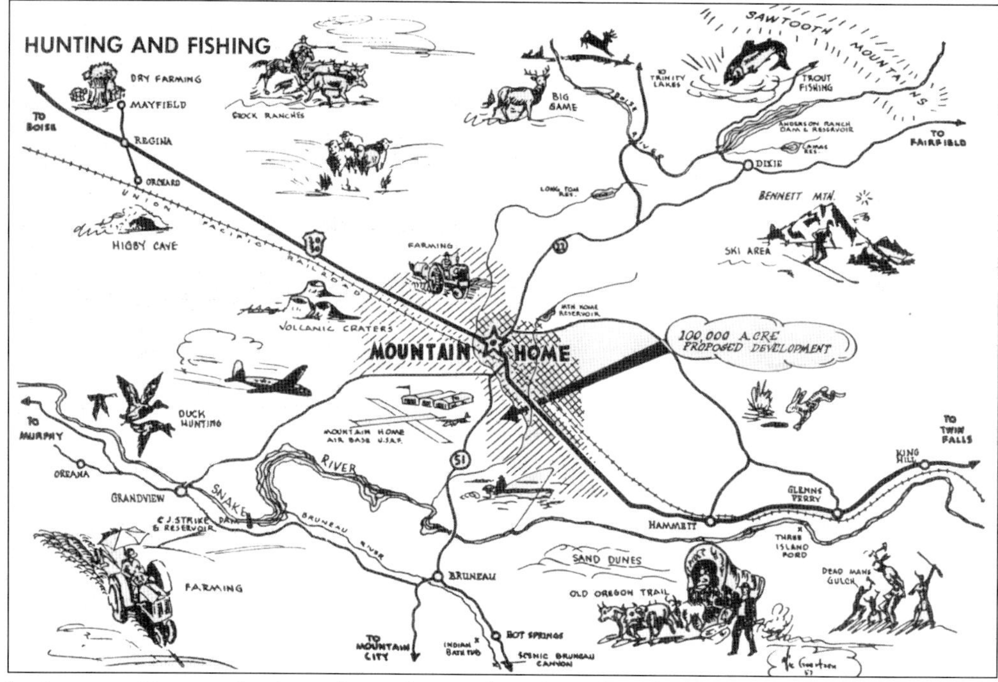

In the annual base guide, the authors advertised just how close the base was to the great outdoors. As with World War II, many airmen from Mountain Home AFB traveled to Boise, but many opted to see more than just the city life. As seen on this map, the base attempted to offer many options for its residents. As an added bonus, the base began its recreational program, taking airmen on trips via the local scenic byways for skiing, fishing, or hunting.

In November 1956, the base announced that it would build a new $341,000 indoor swimming pool. At 80 by 60 feet, the pool would contain enough water to refresh its patrons on even the hottest of summer days. Due to weather delays, it took over two years to build, but it is still being used in 2007.

A proud father and ardent coach talks to his peewee football team during a time-out. During the 1950s, the base became a community for families and new houses were built as well as new recreational facilities. This altered the mind-set of the base from being a home for men during World War II to a home for families during the 1950s.

Members of the Silver Sage riding club pose for a quick photograph in 1960. These avid horseback riders met at the Silver Sage service club but had stables built southeast of the Shell family housing area.

A bagger helps this lady load her car while her daughter plays on the railing. The commissary has always been viewed as the one of the golden cows of military benefits. Its lower prices allowed families living on military incomes to afford the luxuries enjoyed by many others. For years, the commissary operated Monday through Saturday, whereas today it is closed on only Monday.

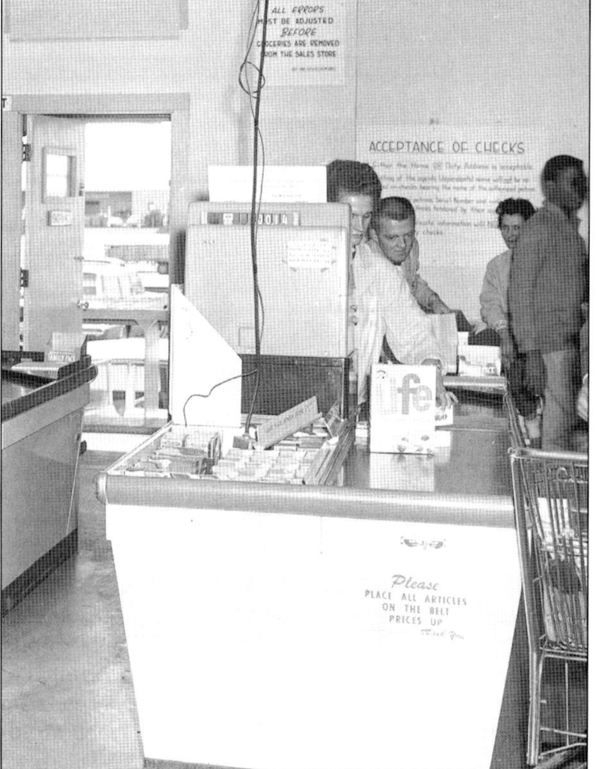

This cashier totals a customer's bill and readies to accept a check.

On March 1, 1960, the Mountain Home AFB strategic alert facility opened for business. Prior to this, the 9th Bomb Wing utilized the World War II–era Hangars 201 and 204 to stage its alert operations. For the ongoing mission, the wing built the alert area a far distance from main base in an attempt to keep prying eyes under control. Lovingly nicknamed the mole hole due to being half underground, the new facility allowed aircrews a place to live while standing on alert duty.

This side view of the B-47 shows just how enormous the jet really was.

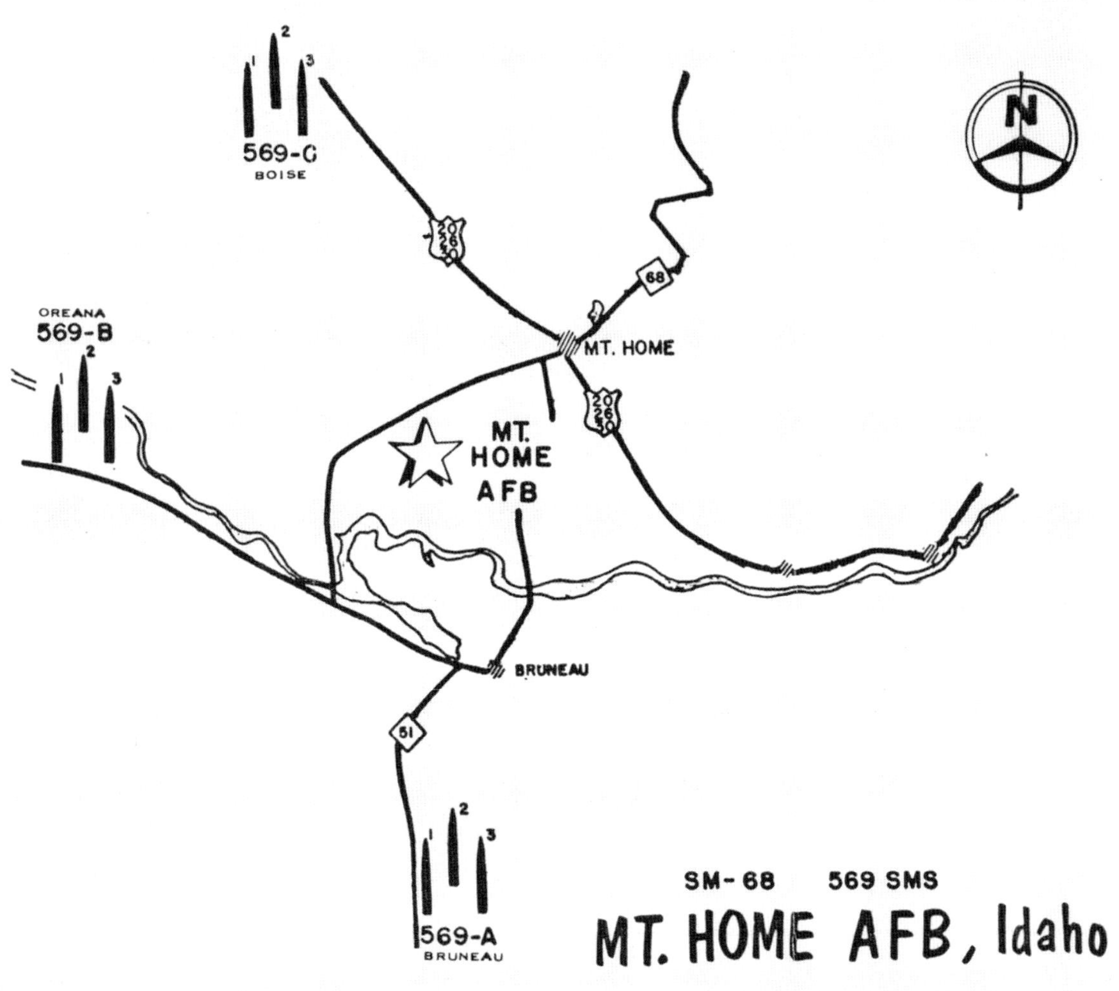

In March 1959, the air force officially announced that Mountain Home AFB had been chosen as one of three bases to house an intercontinental ballistic missile (ICBM) system. Kaiser–Raymond–Macco–Puget Sound, the prime contractor, established a central office in the town of Mountain Home and began work to build three separate sites. Complex A, known as the Bruneau site, was located 26 air miles south of the airbase. Complex B, known as the Oreana site (later named the Orchard site), was located 20 air miles west of the base. Complex C, known as the Boise site, was located 21 air miles north of the base. Each site would occupy approximately 35 acres and would house three Titan missile silos 42 feet in diameter and 14 stories deep. The three missile silos would be connected with an underground complex of living and working quarters. One year after the announcement, Idaho governor Robert E. Smylie turned the first spadeful of dirt at the Orchard site, officially opening construction on Mountain Home's Titan missile complexes.

This overhead shot taken in February 1961 shows the progress of the Oreana site. Here the three missile silos and the domed control facility are clearly visible. Eventually workers would cover the area with dirt, making the site invisible from the air. This protected the site from prying eyes and, most importantly, from a Russian nuclear strike.

This close-up shot shows one of three missile silos in the last phases of construction. To begin building the complex, the contractor conducted open-cut excavation at each site. In this early stage of construction, the contractor learned that the excavation process would be much more difficult at site A than at site C. For this reason, the air force reversed the scheduled completion dates, with site C being finished first and site A being last.

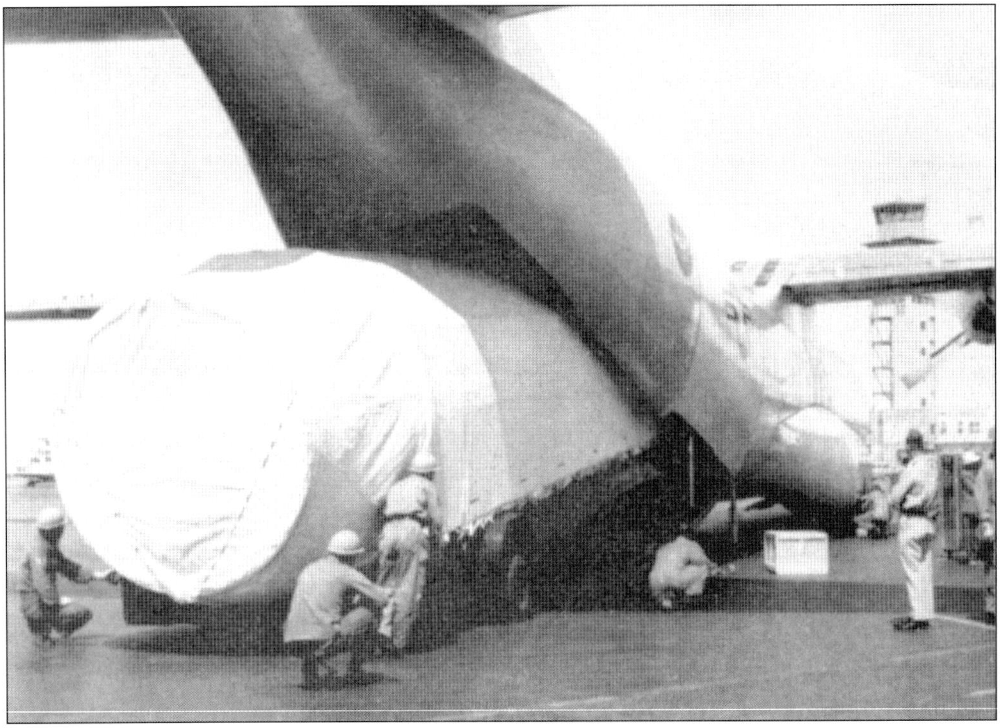

On Friday, April 13, 1962, the first Titan missile arrived at Mountain Home AFB. During a luncheon ceremony, Col. Harmon Burns, the site activation commander, announced that the missile's arrival also signaled the air force's formal acceptance of the Orchard complex. After days of inspections, the missile was convoyed to its new home and lowered into the missile shaft.

After undergoing extensive missile pre checks and a lengthy convoy, the first Mountain Home AFB missile was loaded into a waiting missile silo. Dozing in a catlike sleep in the Mountain Home desert, it was a symbol of the country's deterrent strength. With the lowering of the missile, many hoped that its peaceful slumber would never be awakened.

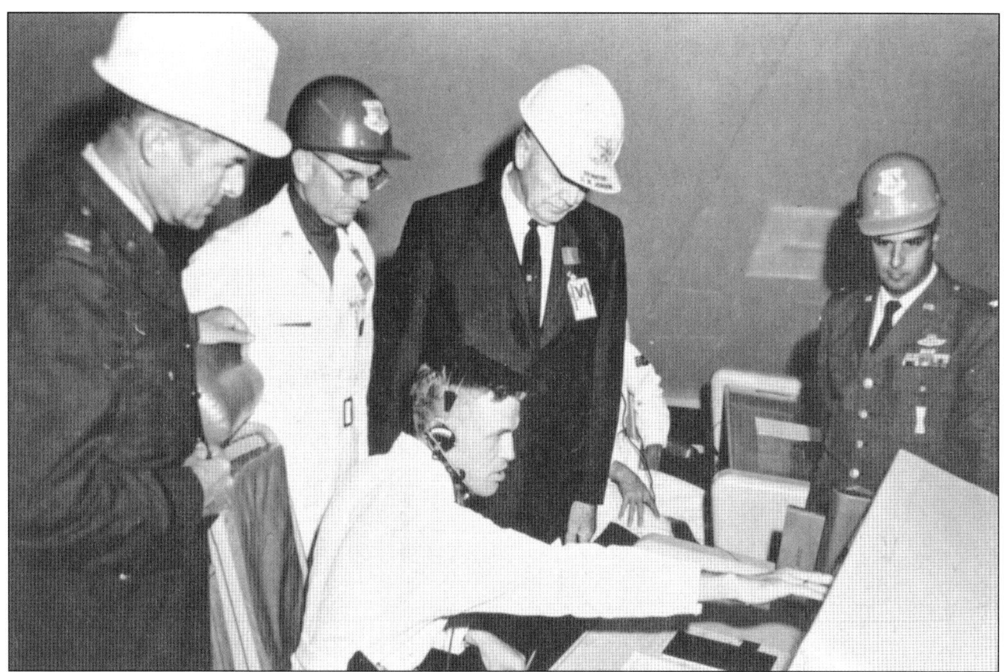

Sen. L. B. Jordan is shown how missile crews would react if called upon. A missile launch demonstration is executed by Capt. Morris K. Fortmann (seated) as (from left to right) Col. Donald T. Smith, 569th Strategic Missile Squadron commander; Maj. William C. Saylor, missile officer; Senator Jordan; and Col. Harmon E. Burns look on.

The missile sites at Mountain Home AFB were active for a very short time. In November 1964, the air force announced it would close the three missile complexes, and by June 1965, all three had been shut down. Here a Titan missile is removed from its silo and readied for transport.

An aerial refueler poses for a quick photograph. To refuel the incoming aircraft, this man took a prone position looking through the window, "flying" the refueling boom down to the awaiting aircraft. Then the two aircraft mated, transferring the fuel through a boom.

This aircrew of the 9th Air Refueling Squadron poses in front of a KC-97 tanker. On September 15, 1954, the squadron received its first KC-97G air refueling tankers. During this period in the 1950s, the 9th helped thrust the air force and Strategic Air Command (SAC) into the early stages of global air capability. Consequently, the 9th's history included numerous deployments to such far-flung locations as French Morocco and Guam.

This was the 9th Bomb Wing's cover photograph for many years. On the left, a B-47 stands alert, while its counterpart, the KC-97, stands by. The newly constructed tower looms in the background.

In December 1954, the 9th Bomb Wing opened its lengthened 12,000-foot runway. Normally the B-47 needed 9,500 feet of the airstrip to takeoff and land safely. This gentleman holds a gauge that clearly illustrates how the runway is beginning to warp.

Hangar 201, a remnant of days gone by, is one of five original World War II hangars on the base. Throughout the years, it has sheltered B-24s, RB-17s, SA-16s, B-29s, and a myriad of modern-day airplanes. Here the hole for a tail section is very clear in the middle of the hangar doors.

To allow school-aged children to catch a few more winks of sleep and to eliminate the long bus ride into the town of Mountain Home, in 1955, the base began building a grade school. Mountain Home School District No. 6 contracted G&M Construction to build the modern facility in January, and in March 1955, the groundbreaking ceremony took place. Eventually the base built a middle school that in 1993 was renamed in honor of a lost Mountain Home pilot, Col. Mark L. Stephenson.

The base club underwent many upgrades in the mid-1950s, but by August 1957, its managers announced a grand reopening. In a newspaper article detailing the event, Barbara Straw, the club's director said, "We feel that MHAFB's service club now will compare with any in SAC insofar as atmosphere, activities and friendly spirit are concerned." During the grand reopening, punch and cookies were served while the 695th Air Force band provided the music for dancing.

In May 1955, the base began construction on its golf course. Previously SAC had generously donated $77,000 of non-appropriated funds to seed the infant project. The funds were used to build a nine-hole course, including the plumbing for the irrigation. The base could not use the funds to build the clubhouse or purchase equipment, so it solicited volunteers from each unit to lend a hand with the manual labor. This is the inside of the first clubhouse.

Three B-47 crew members walk back to base operations after a successful mission. The base liked to adorn its aircraft with thanks to the local community, but it also sponsored esprit de corps through its own nose art. Here Aircraft 2348 sports a "Grow with the 9th" tag on its nose.

A crew chief leans out the window of a KC-97 as the aircraft tug begins to pull forward. In June 1966, the 9th Air Refueling Squadron, as well as the 9th Bomb Wing, departed Mountain Home AFB headed for its new home, Beale AFB.

Three

TAC ATTACK

On January 1, 1966, Tactical Air Command (TAC) took control of Mountain Home AFB and assigned the 67th Tactical Reconnaissance Wing as the host unit. The 67th flew RF-4C and conducted photographic, visual, radar, and thermal reconnaissance operations. In May 1966, shortly after its arrival, the 67th added RF-4C replacement training to its mission, training aircrews for assignment to overseas units. Two years later, the unit also became responsible for tactical fighter operations with the June 1968 addition of a squadron of F-4D Phantoms. This fighter mission lasted until November 1970, when the TAC reassigned the F-4D forces.

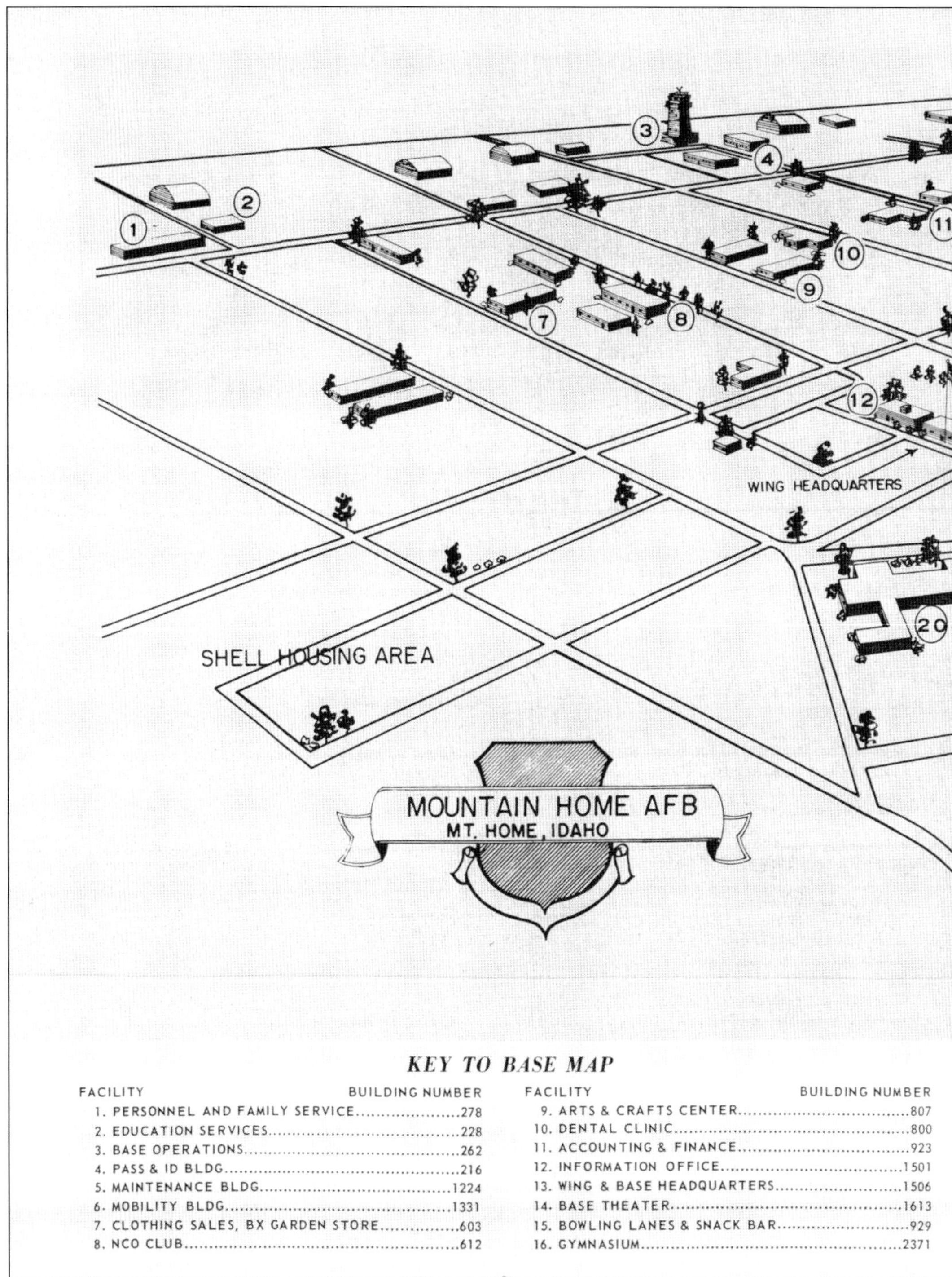

This aerial map taken from a 1966 Mountain Home AFB base guide shows the progress of the post since its opening in 1943. To say that the majority of the construction took place during the 1950s would be an understatement. Under SAC's control, the base grew from a dusty airstrip into a community fit for the new air force. In later years, those who had been stationed at

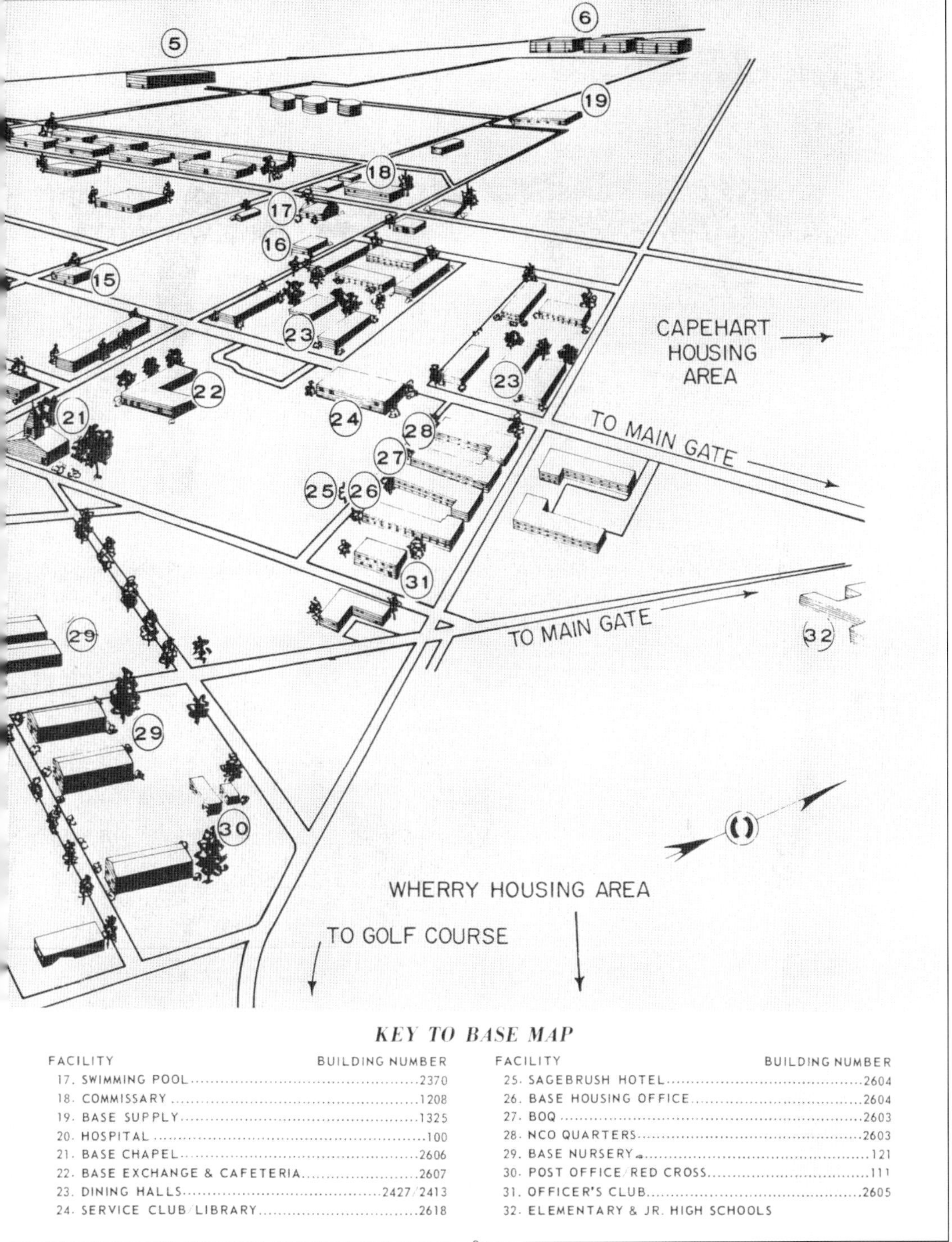

KEY TO BASE MAP

FACILITY	BUILDING NUMBER
17. SWIMMING POOL	2370
18. COMMISSARY	1208
19. BASE SUPPLY	1325
20. HOSPITAL	100
21. BASE CHAPEL	2606
22. BASE EXCHANGE & CAFETERIA	2607
23. DINING HALLS	2427/2413
24. SERVICE CLUB/LIBRARY	2618

FACILITY	BUILDING NUMBER
25. SAGEBRUSH HOTEL	2604
26. BASE HOUSING OFFICE	2604
27. BOQ	2603
28. NCO QUARTERS	2603
29. BASE NURSERY	121
30. POST OFFICE/RED CROSS	111
31. OFFICER'S CLUB	2605
32. ELEMENTARY & JR. HIGH SCHOOLS	

Mountain Home during World War II did not recognize the base upon their return. For one, the streets had been expanded from just A and B Streets running north to south to a gambit of new intersections. Second, the tar paper shacks had been demolished, and in their place new, modern facilities existed.

Phineas Phantom, the mascot for the RF-4C Phantom II, appeared in the base newspaper on a regular basis. With the arrival of TAC and the F-4, the base quickly adapted the phantom as a motif throughout the base. The base newspaper was renamed the *Phantom Photogram*, while the remnants of the SAC era were stripped and replaced with those of TAC.

A group of RF-4Cs sit on the Mountain Home flight line as the sun goes down over the silver sage.

The cover from the 1966 Mountain Home AFB base guide shows two maintainers working on an RF-4C camera. The main mission of the RF-4C was to photograph the enemy's holdings and return to base with the undeveloped film. Afterwards technicians would develop the film, revealing the enemy's secrets.

Two RF-4Cs taxi down the Mountain Home flight line in preparation for takeoff and then a deployment to Vietnam. As part of the 11th Tactical Reconnaissance Squadron, Maj. Mark L. Stephenson deployed to Vietnam. During his time, he flew 94 combat missions as well as 6 combat support missions. On April 29, 1967, he and his WSO (weapons system officer), 1st Lt. Gary Sigler, failed to return after a mission. On September 9, 1993, the base renamed the middle school in his honor.

On September 14, 1943, First Security Bank of Idaho opened a branch at Mountain Home Army Air Field. Through it, base personnel could open checking and savings accounts and purchase war bonds, cashier's checks, traveler's checks, and bank money orders.

After the war, the bank moved out of the World War II building and into a trailer. Over the years, the trailer was adapted and remodeled. In February 2001, Wells Fargo merged with First Security Bank of Idaho, and the stagecoach moniker became a familiar site on the base.

Shown is a view of the base chapel in the late 1960s. This church is still in use today but has been extensively remodeled.

Chapel II, or as it was better know, Freedom Chapel, served Mountain Home AFB for many years. In the late 1980s, the chapel was relegated to serving only special needs like wedding and gospel services. Because of this, the military planned to destroy the structure, but in 1994, the contractor hired to tear the building down gave it to the Abundant Life Church in Mountain Home. It now sits on Air Base Road on the way to Mountain Home AFB.

Aldo Panzieri snapped this photograph of the 67th Tactical Reconnaissance Wing as it conducted a pass in review on the Mountain Home AFB flight line. This was part of the Armed Forces Day celebration in 1967.

Thousands of Idahoans converged on Mountain Home AFB for the annual Armed Forces Day celebration. Here a crowd stands in front of a Military Airlift Command C-141 Starlifter. Prior to the airplane landing, it conducted a mock airborne assault, and airborne troops jumped from the cargo plane and landed in an area around the flight line.

This photograph taken by an orbiting plane shows how much the base had evolved since 1943, though the World War II hangars are very clear. In the upper center of the photograph, the Wherry housing is unmistakable.

This is the Mountain Home AFB main gate as it appeared in 1969. By this point, the volcanic rock and wood planks had been abandoned and replaced with modern lap siding and asphalt shingles. To the right is the visitors' center.

The 67th's stay at Mountain Home was very short lived. In July 1971, the RF-4Cs departed Mountain Home as a new unit, the 347th Tactical Fighter Wing, arrived at Mountain Home and replaced the 67th as the host unit. The RF-4C mission disbanded, and Mountain Home began to receive the F-111F. The 347th also had a short stay at Mountain Home, as the 366th Tactical Fighter Wing—or as they are better known, the Gunfighters—arrived on October 31, 1972. As the 366th absorbed the assets of the 347th, its original three squadrons of World War II heritage (389th, 390th, and 391st) arrived to conduct F-111F operations. With the departure of the 67th, Phineas packed his bags and left Mountain Home forever.

Four

The Gunfighters

On May 24, 1943, the Army Air Forces activated the 366th Fighter Group at Richmond Army Air Base, Virginia. The group's three squadrons, the 389th, 390th, and 391st, trained with the P-47 Thunderbolt for an impending deployment to the European theater. The group first trained at Bluethenthal Field, North Carolina, before returning to Richmond. Seen in this photograph, a group of pilots pose around a P-47 while training at Myrtle Beach, South Carolina. In December 1943, the group returned to Richmond for final staging before transport to Europe. The overseas move began on December 17, with the group traveling to Boston to await transportation. The ship carrying the 366th, the *Empress of Australia*, left Boston for England on December 31, 1943. Ten days later, the group arrived at Membury, England, and began receiving its aircraft. After some in-theater training, the group moved to Thruxton, England, to begin its combat operations.

Prior to moving overseas, the 366th Fighter Group trained at the gunnery range at Wrightsville Beach, North Carolina. Here they hone their skills on strafing the ground and shooting streamers pulled behind another airplane.

After a training flight at the Wrightsville gunnery range, Capt. John H. Pease of the 389th Fighter Squadron takes a look at the streamer he had been firing on. He learned that out of 200 shots fired, he had hit the streamer 60 times.

A few days after D-day, June 6, 1944, the 366th moved across the English Channel and set up operations in France at landing strip A-1. This move complimented the unit's ability to wage war, as it no longer needed to carry extra fuel tanks and in their place could carry bombs.

When the 366th arrived in the theater, for a very short time it escorted B-17 Flying Fortresses flying deep into Germany. As the Flying Fortresses journeyed deeper, the P-47 ran out of range. As an alternate mission, the aircrews began to conduct close air support. In this photograph, a P-47 pilot is providing column cover for an allied tank unit.

Col. Harold Norman Holt assumed command of the 366th Fighter Group on May 22, 1944, and commanded the unit through its toughest days. He always led from the front, never asking his men to do something he himself would not do. This is a 9th Air Force–directed charcoal rendering of Colonel Holt.

Colonel Holt kept a daily journal before he left the United States but quickly lost track of time after the invasion of Normandy. As a leader aware of the importance of history, he wrote many articles on his experiences and had them published in various magazines. This is the cover from his unpublished manuscript detailing the experiences of the 366th in World War II.

Colonel Holt poses in front of his steed, the "Magic Carpet." When he arrived in England, he chose aircraft 42-76516 as his personal plane and flew it into combat for the first time on March 7, 1944. Before Colonel Holt entered the military, he ran a carpet store, and because of this, he christened his aircraft the Magic Carpet. By the end of the war, the aircraft had been flown on 175 missions without an abort.

Capt. Neil D. Stanley from the 391st Fighter Squadron named his aircraft "Daddy Rabbit." The markings on the side of the P-47 denote missions flown as well as the type of targets he had destroyed. Seen here, he had destroyed four tanks and damaged five trains. Crew chiefs normally painted these symbols on their aircraft to build esprit de corps among the men.

Some of the unsung heroes of the war pose in front of a P-47. These transportation troops were responsible for the unit's vehicles as well as moving the unit forward as they hopped from base to base. Whereas the pilots climbed into their aircraft and flew to a new base, the personnel left behind depended on these chaps to get them there.

Pictured is the unofficial World War II emblem of the 391st Fighter Squadron. Maj. Sheldon S. Brinson requested an emblem be created that captured the essence of his unit. It is unknown who actually created this moniker, but it is classic World War II humor. The cow has a 500-pound bomb in its tail, and lightening shoots from its nostrils while its udders spew .50-caliber bullets.

In January 1953, the air force reactivated the 366th as the 366th Fighter-Bomber Wing and stationed the unit at Alexandria Air Base, Louisiana. To build esprit de corps, the wing commander requested the unit develop an emblem to symbolize its strength. The men choose a mighty tiger as the centerpiece, with the words *Audentes Fortuna Juvat* in the scroll. Translated, it means "fortune favors the bold."

Maj. John B. England served with the 362nd Fighter Squadron during World War II and became a triple ace with 17.5 aerial victories. After the war, he served as the 389th Fighter-Bomber Squadron commander from October 31, 1953, until November 17, 1954. During a routine mission near Toul, France, he crashed his F-84F. In his honor, the U.S. Air Force renamed Alexandria AFB in Louisiana, England AFB.

The maintenance personnel working on F-84Fs adopted this emblem in 1954. Its design symbolized the unit's mission of caring for the wing's aircraft. At the time, the F-84F was a very sophisticated airplane that carried nuclear-tipped missiles.

During a deployment to Italy, several F-84Fs underwent repairs in a makeshift maintenance dock. While deployed to the European theater, the F-84Fs sat alert with their nuclear-tipped missiles loaded and ready to go.

In August 1957, the 389th Fighter-Bomber Squadron commander, Maj. Joseph P. Kelsey, led a contingent of 20 Republic F-84Fs and 190 personnel to Aviano Air Base, Italy, where his unit conducted a one-month standby alert test. Here, seconds after the scramble signal, crew members dash from the alert hangar to their waiting aircraft.

After a short inactivation at the end of the 1950s, the air force reactivated the 390th and redesignated it as the 390th Tactical Fighter Squadron. The unit stood on alert duty while stationed at Chaumont Air Base, France, until July 1963, when it transferred to Holloman AFB, New Mexico. In preparation for its deployment to Vietnam, the unit traded in its F-84Fs and reequipped with the F-4C. After a training flight in the F-4, Captain Hall holds the 390th's scroll.

This unidentified 390th pilot climbs into the cockpit of his F-84F.

During World War II, the 390th Fighter Squadron adopted the nickname "the Boars." Maj. Joseph S. Michalowski served as the unit commander in 1956 and 1957. At that time, the unit's memorabilia was put on display at the 390th's bar, including a boar's head from World War II. After the 390th inactivated in April 1959, many of these items disappeared. After the unit arrived at Holloman AFB, then-Colonel Michalowski, along with his sons, returned the boar to its rightful owners.

In August 1965, the 366th adopted this emblem. With all military emblems, there is significance in each element. Here the wedge is symbolic of the victorious wedge battle formation. The escutcheon—the small inner shield—commemorates the Distinguished Unit Citation and the campaign credits the 366th Fighter Group and its squadrons earned during World War II. The flight symbols represent aircraft and indicate worldwide deployment capability and a lightning punch. The emblem bears the air force colors, ultramarine blue and air force yellow, and the national colors red, white, and blue.

On March 20, 1966, the 366th Tactical Fighter Wing deployed to Vietnam. In the beginning, the air force stationed the unit at Phan Rang Air Base, but by October, it had moved to Da Nang Air Base, South Vietnam. From there, the wing operated its F-4C Phantoms while acting as the host unit for the base.

Aircrew from the 390th pose in front of "Naughty Nora." For a time during the Vietnam War, nose art returned to grace the air force's aircraft. Also very clear in this photograph is the coveted Shaky Spook patch, indicating that in February 1968, the nickname "the Gunfighters" had been fully adopted.

Lt. Lance Peter Sijan holds a very special place in the 366th's history, as he is the only Medal of Honor recipient in the unit and the first Air Force Academy graduate to earn the honor. Lieutenant Sijan and his squadron commander, Lt. Col. John Armstrong, were shot down during a mission over the Ho Chi Mihn Trail. Sijan miraculously survived the ejection then evaded capture for 46 days. He died in captivity, and for his heroism and strict adherence to the Code of Conduct, the military awarded him with the Medal of Honor. (Photograph courtesy of the Air Force Academy.)

After the 366th missed several opportunities to kill enemy MiGs, its commander, Col. Jones E. Bolt, requested his maintainers rig a jet with the SUU-16 gun pod. Slinging the gun pod had little effect on the aircraft, so after a month of testing, the wing flew its first combat missions with the new gun pod on May 12. Two days later, two crews, consisting of Maj. Jim Hargrove and 1st Lt. Steve Demuth and Capt. Jim Craig and 1st Lt. Steve Talley each shot down a MiG-17 with the gun. Between April 23 and June 5, 1967, 366th crews shot down 11 MiGs—4 with the gun. No other unit scored as many kills in such a short period throughout the war. This feat earned the 366th its nickname, the Gunfighters.

A "Load Toad" inspects a SUU-23 gun pod before loading it on the belly of a waiting F-4C. The driver would use the MJ-1 "Jammer" to move the gun pod into position under the aircraft, and then a second person would attach the device to the aircraft.

After the wing had downed several MiGs with its externally mounted Gatling guns, many other units throughout Vietnam began to refer to the 366th as the Gunfighters. This moniker quickly caught on, and an emblem soon arrived on Colonel Bolt's desk. The artist christened the emblem the "Shaky Spook." The Spook, the mascot of the F-4 Phantom, held a SUU-16 gun pod that caused him to shake uncontrollably. Colonel Bolt adopted the concept art as the unit's unofficial insignia and ordered it applied to all wing aircraft.

As the Gunfighters became better known for their accomplishments in Vietnam, they were called upon more and more. Partly as a joke, the aircrews began to hand out calling cards when paying a quick visit to local units. This version was handed out by Maj. Gen. J. R. Spalding, who commanded the 366th from February to July 1971.

Five

Idaho, Home of the Gunfighters

With operations in Vietnam coming to a close, the air force chose to move the 366th's designator to Mountain Home AFB. On October 31, 1972, the Gunfighter designator arrived at Mountain Home AFB and absorbed the assets of the 347th. The 366th's original three squadrons of World War II heritage (389th, 390th, and 391st) also arrived at this time to conduct F-111F operations. This continued until 1977. In order to modernize its European forces, the air force decided to send the F-111F aircraft from Mountain Home to the wing at RAF Lakenheath, England. The F-4 aircraft from Lakenheath went to Nellis AFB, Nevada, while the 366th received F-111A aircraft from Nellis. This three-way swap, code-named Operation Ready Switch, took place from October 1976 through August 1977.

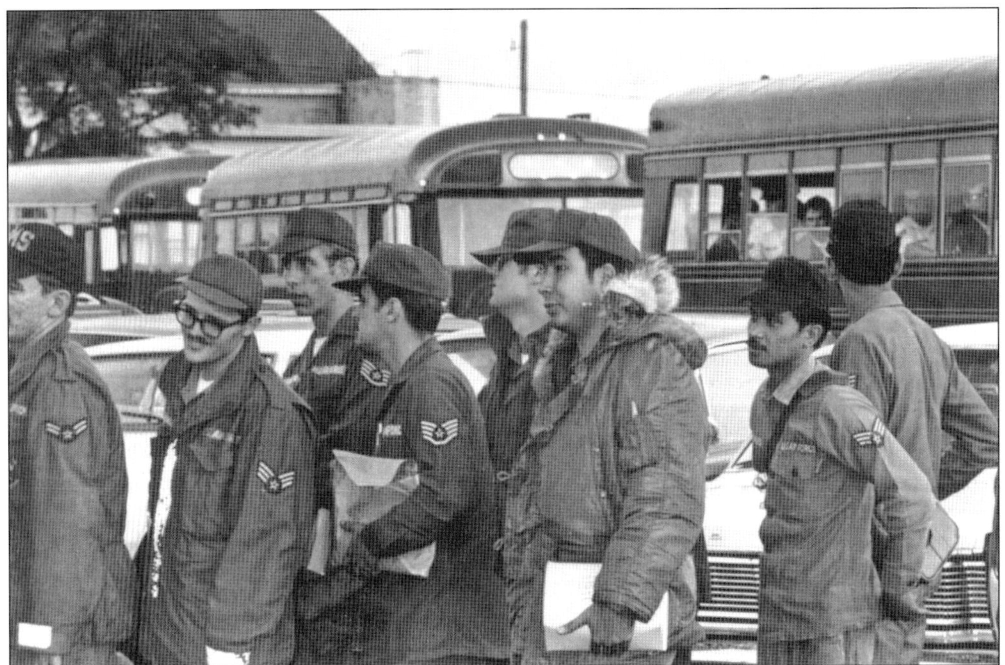

Operations continued unchanged at Mountain Home for several years, with the 366th Tactical Fighter Wing conducting training in the F-111F and maintaining combat readiness. The wing had the opportunity to test this readiness in August 1976, when a border incident in Korea prompted the United States to augment its military contingent in South Korea as a show of force. Here support personnel board buses that will take them to waiting cargo aircraft.

The 366th was tasked to deploy a squadron of 20 F-111 fighters as a part of this buildup, with the detachment reaching Korea only 31 hours after receiving launch notification. Tensions eased shortly afterward, and the detachment gradually returned to Mountain Home from mid-September through early October 1976. The quick response to the emergency tasking earned the wing an Air Force Outstanding Unit Award for Operation Paul Bunyan.

Col. John L. Pickett, 366th Tactical Fighter Wing commander, discusses various aspects of Ready Switch operations with Col. Robert E. Messerli, the 48th Tactical Fighter Wing commander from RAF Lakenheath, England.

A corrosion specialist paints over the Tactical Air Command emblem while applying a fresh coat of paint. "MO," representing Mountain Home AFB, was removed and replaced with "LN," representing the 48th Tactical Fighter Wing at RAF Lakenheath, England.

A pair of F-111s flies across the Idaho sky. This was a very familiar sight until the air force began phasing the F-111 from its inventory. In July 1991, the last F-111 left Mountain Home bound for the bone yard. In their place, the air force stood up the composite wing at Mountain Home.

To stimulate community relations, the wing often invited local dignitaries to view the F-111 Aardvark. The Gunfighters created a dog-and-pony show, surrounding the F-111 with various laser-guided weapons as well as the sundry equipment used to repair and operate the aircraft.

In the spring of 1973, 1st Lt. A. M. Crowe, the vice president of the Junior Officer Council, welcomed Maj. Dorman B. Moose Jr. as he climbed down from an F-100. Major Moose delivered the F-100 to Mountain Home as part of a project to display aircraft from the wing's history. For several years, the base displayed the aircraft in front of the 390th's squadron operations building, but in 1987, the Gunfighters mounted an effort to consolidate the base's displays into one large heritage park.

In January 1994, after the construction of the airpark had been underway for some time, Staff Sergeant Mark Bucher took this photograph. The cold silver sage blended very well with the all-metal finish on the F-100.

As in the past, in September 1978, the base participated in Air Force Appreciation Day in downtown Mountain Home. The 366th Tactical Fighter Wing commander, Col. Von R. Christiansen, serves potato salad to an eager customer. It is very common for the wing commander and his commanders to serve food during the event.

During Air Force Appreciation Day, dignitaries from all over the state converge on the tiny town of Mountain Home to play their role in the annual parade. Here Gov. Cecil Andrus and his wife ride in the back of a car and greet the onlookers. It is very common for the parade to last more than an hour and for those on the floats to toss candy and goodies to those watching.

These gentlemen prepare chicken for sale during Air Force Appreciation Day. The community of Mountain Home is heavily sprinkled with retired personnel from the base. For this reason, the retirees play a large role in the annual event.

A member from Mountain Home AFB serves up more potato salad. Air Force Appreciation Day events begin the Friday before. The leadership from the base arrives at Carl Miller Park and participates in a corn-shucking contest. Each year, the contestants attempt to break the record from the year before. Saturday begins with the large parade, and then the town gathers at the park for a day of music, food, and fun.

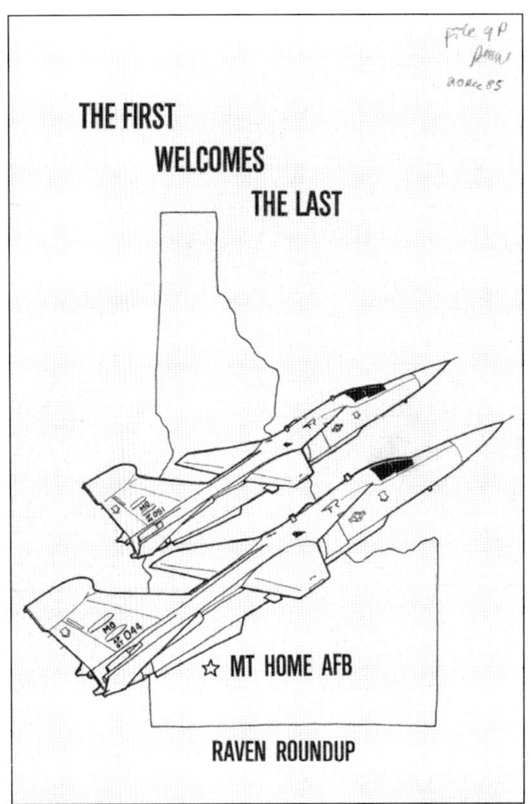

On November 5, 1981, the first EF-111, serial number 66-051, touched down at Mountain Home AFB. Between that time and December 1985, the 388th Electronic Combat Squadron, then later the 390th Electronic Combat Squadron, accepted 28 Ravens into the nest. On December 11, 1985, the Gunfighters celebrated as the 390th accepted the last EF-111, serial number 67-044, into the fold, thus becoming the first operational EF-111 squadron in the air force.

This photograph of the EF-111 clearly illustrates the aircraft's swing wing. The aviation company Grumman Aerospace Corporation adapted the F-111 airframe and created the EF-111. The mission of the EF-111 was to operate at Mach 2-plus, jamming any and all electronic enemy signals. It carried no ordnance and had no way to defend itself.

When the 366th arrived in October 1972, it assumed the F-111 mission. After Operation Ready Switch, the wing began to integrate the EF-111 mission into its fold. To represent this, the maintainers erected a large-scale model of each airframe in front of the base headquarters.

Throughout the 1980s, the 389th Tactical Fighter Training Squadron instructed thousands of pilots and weapons systems officers in the operation of the F-111. In this photograph, a recently graduated class hams it up for the camera.

This female from the Security Police Squadron demonstrates how her canine can jump over an obstacle. The Security Police Squadron demonstrated these capabilities during air shows or when dignitaries visited the base. This gave the community a better understanding of their mission.

Though they are laughable by today's standards, in the mid-1980s, the Communication Squadron touted these capabilities as being cutting edge. The majority of data was stored on large tape reels versus the hard drives used today. These machines took up large amounts of space and by today's standards were very slow.

In January 1979, a maintenance crew tows an F-111, serial number 0-22, down the streets of Mountain Home AFB. The story of the F-111 involved the efforts of many people, including Capt. Bill Swan of the 389th Tactical Fighter Training Squadron and many other members of the Base Junior Officer Council. Chapters in the story entailed the refurbishment of the airplane that arrived in pieces from Wright Patterson AFB, Ohio. Led by Senior Master Sergeant Philip E. Hasty Jr., the aircraft was restored to its present condition.

On September 7, 1979, the 366th Tactical Fighter Wing commander, Col. Von. R. Christiansen, along with the former commander, Gen. John L. Pickitt, oversaw the dedication of the F-111 memorial. In that same ceremony, Mountain Home mayor Nelson H. Olds proclaimed the day "Spirit of Idaho Day" in the town of Mountain Home. The memorial honored the memories of F-111 flight crews lost in Southeast Asia.

The 724th Air Force Band from McChord Air Force Base, Washington, provided music for the ceremony, from the national anthem to a variety of stirring martial music.

At the conclusion, Col. Von. R. Christiansen, 366th Tactical Fighter Wing commander, directed the attention of the audience to an F-111A flyover. This is the U.S. Air Force's traditional salute to its departed members.

This overhead shot at a Mountain Home AFB open house shows two F-111As proudly on display. To show the variance in the wing sweep, one aircraft has its wings swept fully back. This was the configuration for flying past Mach 1.

Another shot of a Mountain Home AFB open house shows the air force demonstration team, the Thunderbirds, taxiing into the show center. The majority of air force air shows center on the Thunderbirds.

This pamphlet contained basic safety information for the Gunfighters deploying to support Operation Desert Storm. Created by the Air Force Inspection and Safety Center, its authors hoped its contents would jog its reader's memories and dust out the cobwebs that had formed from years of no war.

The wing deployed its flagship, "The Spirit of Idaho," as part of the Gunfighter contingent for Operation Desert Storm.

(U) The 366th Wing's flagship EF-111A, "The Spirit of Idaho."

(U) Mission markings on 390 ECS (P) aircraft. At this point in the war, the aircraft had flown 18 missions. Note the Desert Storm logo under the windscreen.

In 1991, the 390th Electronic Combat Squadron deployed to Saudi Arabia in support of Operation Desert Storm. The unit escorted strike packages into Iraq, jamming enemy radar and surface-to-air missile sites. At the end of the war, the 390th boasted an impressive record of 875 missions. In this photograph, a 390th maintainer poses for his hero shot. Note the mission markings under the canopy as well as the Desert Storm logo.

Two EF-111 Ravens sit outside their hangars. While deployed to Saudi Arabia, the 390th Electronic Combat Squadron combined with 48th Tactical Fighter Wing from RAF Lakenheath, England. Nonetheless, the 390th Electronic Combat Squadron proudly displayed their unit's heraldry.

The 390th Electronic Combat Squadron gathered for a hero shot before leaving the Saudi desert. During their support of Operation Desert Storm, the squadron flew 875 sorties protecting coalition aircrews as they decimated the Iraqi war machine.

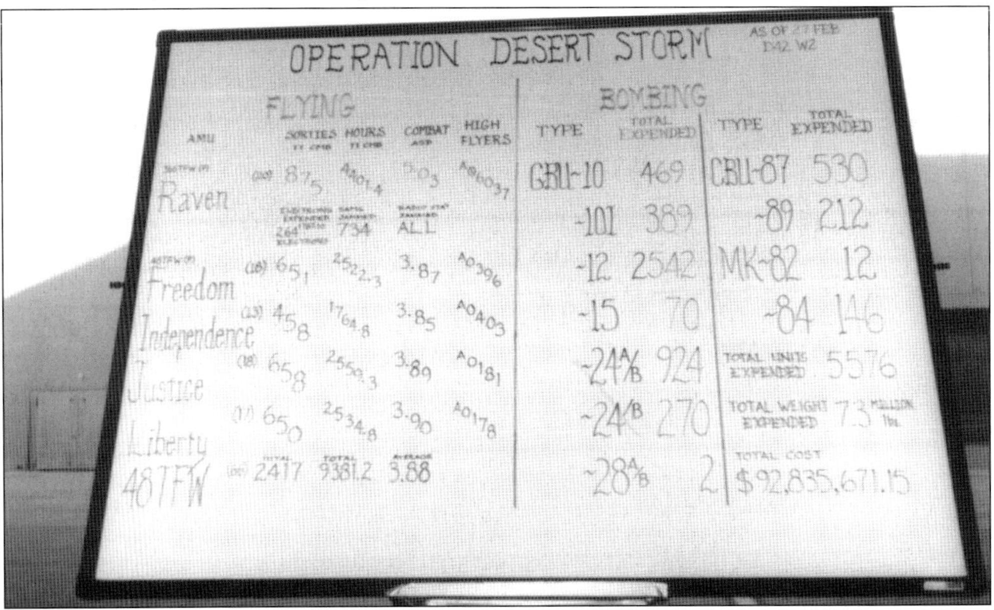

This photograph captured the results of the F-111/EF-111 mission board for Operation Desert Storm. On February 27, 1991, the day the war came to an end, the Ravens had flown 875 sorties for a total of 44,014 hours. Sadly, during the war, the 390th lost an aircrew. Pilot Capt. Douglas L. Bradt and EWO (electronic warfare officer) Capt. Paul R. Eichenlaub crashed their EF-111A, 66-0023, into terrain while maneuvering to evade a perceived enemy aircraft threat. It was the only EF-111A lost during combat, the only loss killing its crew, and one of just three EF-111s lost in the plane's history.

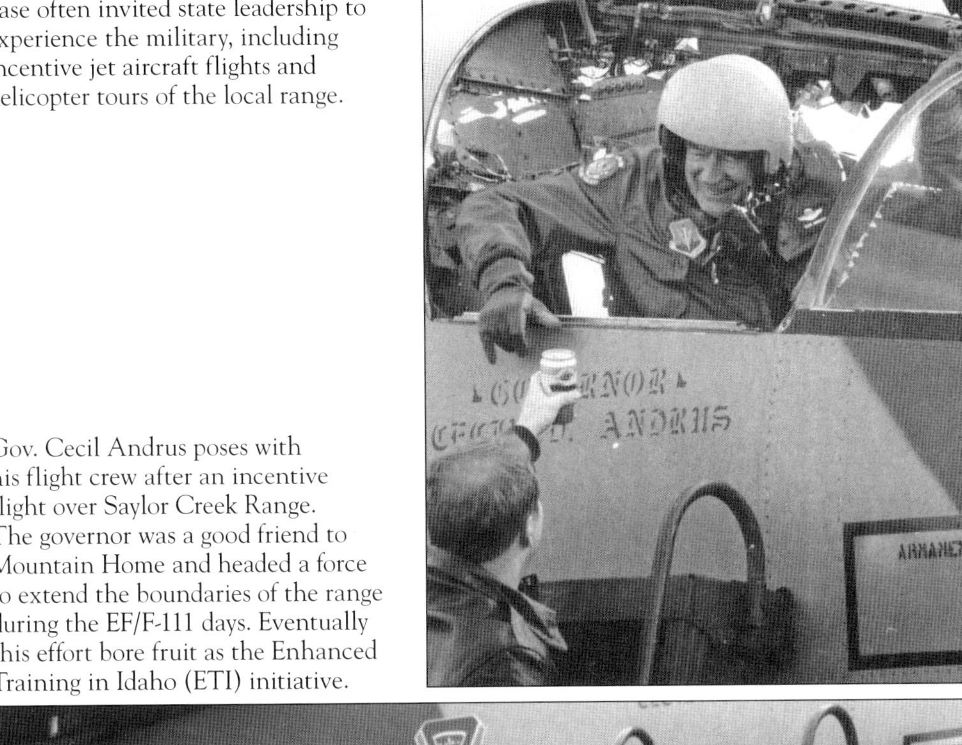

After a short flight above Mach 2 while just feet off the ground, Gov. Cecil Andrus readily accepts a beverage from a fellow pilot. The base often invited state leadership to experience the military, including incentive jet aircraft flights and helicopter tours of the local range.

Gov. Cecil Andrus poses with his flight crew after an incentive flight over Saylor Creek Range. The governor was a good friend to Mountain Home and headed a force to extend the boundaries of the range during the EF/F-111 days. Eventually this effort bore fruit as the Enhanced Training in Idaho (ETI) initiative.

Pilots of the 390th Electronic Combat Squadron consult a large map of the Saylor Creek Range and plan a daily mission.

Recent graduates of the F-111 training program run by the 389th Tactical Fighter Training Squadron pose on a defunct M-113 armored transport. These types of vehicles dotted the Saylor Creek range and acted as targets for the aircrews.

The Mountain Home AFB main gate in the late 1980s looked modern and professional. With its sharp security forces personnel checking identification and saluting smartly, those not familiar with military life were intimidated. By this point in the base's evolution, trees had begun to mature and shade the area. Grass had sprouted and calmed the desert winds, keeping the dust at bay. Although the gate had been upgraded, it continued to serve the same purpose: to be the first line of defense for the base.

When visiting dignitaries landed at Mountain Home, the first building they visited was the base operations. This building had been erected under the 1950 construction period, when SAC still ran the base. Although other programs fell behind in schedule, the base operations building was finished on time.

The 366th Honor Guard prepares to lead the Boise Memorial Day Parade. These young men and women appeared often in the Mountain Home parades, but to star in the Boise event was a treat for not only the airmen, but also for the civilians.

Armed Force Appreciation Day has always been an event where the local community and the base get together and celebrate. From corn-shucking contests to dancing in the streets, the military and local populace always looked forward to the event. The two days of celebration begin with a large parade, and in this photograph, a very proud F-111 pilot drives a miniature version of his aircraft.

After the arrival of the F-100 in the spring of 1973, the plane sat in front of the 390th's headquarters. Some time later, an F-84F arrived and sat in open storage for years. With the construction of the new wing headquarters building complete, an effort was put in motion to build a heritage park. In that park, the wing would place aircraft that it had flown over the years. Here crews hoist the F-100 up to its new home.

In 1988, the wing procured a dilapidated F-4C and refurbished the aircraft. A short time later, they placed it at the helm of the airpark in honor of Capt. Lance Sijan. Capt. Lance Sijan is the Gunfighters' only Medal of Honor recipient as well as the first U.S. Air Force Academy graduate to receive the honor.

On September 18, 1992, the 366th Fighter Wing invited former members of the 490th Bomb Group to a ceremony highlighting that unit's achievements during World War II. Close to 300 personnel of the 490th arrived at Mountain Home and did not recognize the base. The men toured the B-24 hangars and commented that the elimination of the tar paper shacks was a definite improvement.

This shot shows the F-84F on display as well as Capt. Lance Peter Sijan's F-4C. The airpark is a highlight of the base for people visiting, because they can see aircraft they might have once worked on or supported.

The quest to place an F-4C in the airpark dates back to October 1980, when the wing commander directed the history office to find a suitable plane for display. For close to eight years, the historian attempted to secure an aircraft to no avail. Finally, with backing from the muscle of several colonels, Technical Sergeant Danny Blue was able to procure F-4C tail number 64-0841. In June 1988, the aircraft arrived at the base, and the corrosion shop went to work repairing any deficiencies and painting it to match the markings of Capt. Lance Peter Sijan's aircraft. This photograph taken in the summer of 2003 by Lisa Mailes shows the real beauty of the airpark. Captain Sijan's aircraft leads the other airplanes that have played a significant role in the unit's history. In September 2003, the 366th renamed Heritage Park Holt Park in honor of the 366th's first combat commander, Col. Harold Norman Holt.

One of the most disturbing air force traditions during a Dining In involves the Grog Bowl. Committee members find a basin—usually a toilet—and fill the bowl with copious amounts of liquor, usually topped off with a Baby Ruth. When a person's name is called, he marches to the Grog Bowl, dips his cup, recites a preplanned speech, and downs the drink in one swift gulp. If he incorrectly completes the task, he is ordered to repeat the process. While the event is voluntary and in good fun, it often leads to very slurred speech followed by extended amounts of embarrassment.

Troy "Air" Myles prepares to slam dunk in a basketball game against the Security Police Squadron. Troy was a member of the hospital team that defeated the security police by an awesome score of 95-26.

Technical Sergeant Floyd Rehkopf pauses during an exercise to survey the scene. The 366th exercises on a regular basis to stay prepared for war. Tech Sergeant Rehkopf wears a chemical ensemble that will protect him from a chemical attack.

A security forces member has her canine run through the obstacle course. The dogs must be able to scale steep obstacles like the one in the background as well as sniff for drugs or bombs.

Over the years, the main gate changed as well as the uniform of the men and women manning the post, but the location always stayed the same. In this photograph, a young security forces guard salutes as he identifies an officer coming through the base portal.

In 1992, the air force formed the composite wing at Mountain Home. As a 911 strike force, the unit consisted of KC-135s, B-1Bs, F-15Es, F-15Cs, and F-16CJs. With this combination of airpower, the 366th could quickly deploy and quell any uprising anywhere in the world. This concept was tested during Operation Enduring Freedom, when the Gunfighters deployed for the first 105 days of the war, dropping more bombs and striking more targets than any other unit.

Initially the 34th Bomb Squadron operated the B-52 from Castle AFB, California, but in 1994, the unit transferred to Ellsworth AFB, South Dakota, and began operating the B-1B. Here the Castle AFB Honor Guard displays the colors during the transition ceremony.

The 366th Composite Wing deployed to Egypt for Bright Star in October 1993. This was an exercise designed to test the unit's ability to deploy as a composite force. It also sent a clear signal to the nation's enemies that the Gunfighters were ready for war.

The 389th Fighter Squadron deployed to Al Undeid Air Base, Qatar, in support of Operation Enduring Freedom. As with most conflicts, as the war raged, nose art began to show up on the jets. This F-16, serial number 91-0413, carried the "OEF Gunfighters" regalia on its side. Staff Sergeant Chad Marks listened to the crew chief and translated his desires into nose art. He penciled the drawings onto the aircraft, then Technical Sergeant Robbie Leist helped color them in.

As part of the composite wing, this B-1B of the 34th Bomb Squadron brought the long reach needed for war. During Operation Enduring Freedom, the unit deployed and employed the newly acquired GBU-31 Joint Direct Attack Munition (JDAM) and devastated Taliban strongholds.

With the 366th deploying to support Operation Enduring Freedom, many unit artists put their talents to work and adorned the squadron aircraft. The 22nd Air Refueling Squadron painted this piece on one of their jets, sending a clear signal of the Gunfighters' intentions after September 11.

Another 389th Fighter Squadron jet shows nose art from Operation Enduring Freedom. Lt. Col. Thomas J. Lawhead, the 389th commander during the conflict, requested that his jet, aircraft 92-3889, have a vulture painted upon it.

The 389th deployed to Al Undeid, Qatar, to support the war on terror. During the deployment, several ground-crew members adorned their aircraft with nose art. Usually applying the art with chalk, each artist used the F-16CJ as his canvas, creating art that built the unit's esprit de corps. In this photograph, the artist has created a scene where the firefighters of September 11 handed the responsibility off to the 389th. This aircraft, serial number 89-0506, along with its pilot, went on to destroy several Taliban strongholds. Chief Master Sergeant Andy Bower sent a photograph of this plane to the New York police and fire departments.

In 2002, the 366th swapped its F-15Es with Elmendorf AFB, Alaska. When the first Elmendorf F-15E arrived, aircrews from the 391st arrived in style, driving their tigermobile. Two units on Mountain Home sport their own squadron cars. Each symbolizes the morale of the unit.

In December 2005, the air force announced that Mountain Home would transition to an all F-15E wing. To do this, the 389th Fighter Squadron sent its F-16CJs to other bases beginning in late 2006. The 390th Fighter Squadron will transition from an F-15C unit to an F-15E unit by 2010. Shown here is the 391st Fighter Squadron "Bold Tigers." Its aircrews have operated the F-15E since the inception of the composite wing and stand as the only relic of that effort.